RETURN UNTO ME

OLD TESTAMENT MESSAGES
OF GOD'S LOVE FOR YOU

OTHER BOOKS AND AUDIOS

BY KERRY MUHLESTEIN

Essential Old Testament Companion

Understanding the Book of Abraham

RETURN
UNTO ME

OLD TESTAMENT MESSAGES
OF GOD'S LOVE FOR YOU

KERRY MUHLESTEIN PH.D.

Covenant Communications, Inc.

Cover image Stairway to the Sun © anneleven

Cover design copyright © 2013 by Covenant Communications, Inc.

Published by Covenant Communications, Inc.
American Fork, Utah

Printed in the United States of America
First Printing: August 2013

19 18 17 16 15 14 13   10 9 8 7 6 5 4 3 2 1

ISBN 978-1-62108-497-6

DEDICATION

To BJ, Tashara, Kaleb, Alexia, Sabrina, and Jacob,
who have taught me so much more
about how much God loves us

Biblical quotes in this text are drawn from the 1611 translation of the Kings James Version (KJV) of the Bible. In those instances where the quotes are not from the KJV, the substituted translation is specifically noted in the text.

ACKNOWLEDGMENTS

I am grateful to many people for helping shape my thoughts and my ability to express them as I wrote this book. The questions my Old Testament students earnestly asked helped me learn what good, intelligent members of the Church wanted to know as they studied the Old Testament and what needs were not being met.

Several people—more than I can mention here—helped me organize and polish this book. Particular thanks goes to S. Kate Lindsay, Kelsey Berteaux, Amy Faust, Lynde Mott, and Jennifer Bischoff. My wife and children taught me so much about what love really means and were so good-humored as I told stories about them in the book. I am also grateful to the editors at Covenant Communications who received this manuscript in a rough form and were able to look through its roughness and see the potential.

When the task became making this into a more beautiful project, my wife, Julianne, poured over the drafts again and again. It would be a much poorer product without her help.

I am especially grateful to the talented and inspired writers of old who understood God, His love, and His way of working with us, and who poured their lives into portraying that for us. I think that in this life we will never fully appreciate what those great prophets and scribes have done for us. I am confident that when we fully come to feel God's love for us and how the Old Testament has guided our lives in ways we never recognized, we will fall on their necks as we weep for joy and gratitude.

—Kerry Muhlestein

TABLE OF CONTENTS

CHAPTER ONE
GOD LOVES US

And the Lord spake unto Enoch, and said unto him: Anoint thine eyes with clay, and wash them, and thou shalt see. And He did so. And He beheld the spirits that God had created; and He beheld also things which were not visible to the natural eye;
(Moses 6:35–36)

Return unto me, and I will return unto you.
(Mal. 3:7)

God Loves Us

MY WIFE ONCE HAD AN experience that applies to us all in a profoundly significant way. She was correcting our five-year-old son, and after telling him what he had done wrong, she added an almost habitual and automated, "I love you." This particular time, though, she realized that he needed something more. Changing her plan, she took the time to talk to him about how much she loved him and how nothing would ever change that. She went through a list, telling him that she would still love him even if he did this or even if he did that.

The conversation ripped him out of his traditional reaction to being corrected. The phrase *I will love you no matter what!* was gripping and startling to him, and he was amazed that his mother would love him despite anything he might do wrong. As she repeated that affirmation, he was transformed and drew closer to her. For some time thereafter he verbally explored the depths and strength of her love. *No matter what* became a meaningful phrase for the two of them.

My son wasn't the only one who was startled. My wife had always assumed our son knew and understood this principle, and she was surprised at the power of their seemingly small dialogue. It changed his outlook of who he was, his understanding of his relationship with his mother, and his perception of what she was doing when she corrected him.

His knowledge of my wife's unconditional and unending love seemed to give him a wonderful hope; he appeared to walk through life a little lighter. Perhaps it eased his worry that his wrong choices might change her feelings toward him—and maybe he no longer felt he had to justify everything he did in order to prevent that change. In a very small way, his knowledge of his mother's love for him demonstrates the effect God's love can have on all of us when we really know how His love works.

I'm not the only one who feels wonder and awe at God's love for us. Nor do I think I'm alone in another reality: sometimes I feel God's love strongly, while at other times I am forced to rely on my memory of that love since I'm not feeling it at the moment. I do know that all of us need to feel God's love and to experience His spiritual arms wrapped around us.

When it comes to relying on the scriptures to capture those feelings, I think it's less common to recognize God's love in the Old Testament. But intensively studying the Old Testament can change the way we experience life. For me, that change comes because of the sweeping message of love I find in the pages of that book. You may have noticed different themes in the Book of Mormon when you have read it quickly. Both my wife and I have had the same experience with the Old Testament as we have either read or listened to it consistently and quickly. When we allow it to flood our lives in this way, and when we see the larger stories swirling around us through this experience, we have both been struck with the continual themes of God's love—the repeated chances He gives His children, the forgiveness He extends to them, and His willingness to always accept them back.

This same effect happens if I delve into this sacred book in a slow, diligent, and scrutinizing manner. I am sometimes overwhelmed by the continual images of God's love for His people as a whole and for each of us individually, no matter what we have done, at all odds and at all costs. I find myself, regardless of where I am or what I am doing, feeling encompassed with a sense of comfort and gratitude for this love. Immersing myself in the Old Testament chases away those moments I do not feel God's love. Instead, I walk around with a deep-seated sense of joy, suffused in a happiness and peace that come only from unceasingly feeling how much God loves me.

This love permeates deep into my soul. It affects the way I see everything, the way I feel about everything, and every desire I have. Even during these times I don't think I'm capable of feeling the true depth of God's love for me; that kind of feeling is beyond my capacity. Yet even the partial view of His love changes me. When I feel God's love in this way, life is fuller, I am more attentive to the Spirit, events and people are more meaningful, and small things bring greater satisfaction. There is nothing I desire more than to keep experiencing this feeling. It consumes me. I feel an overwhelming desire to do anything that will enable me to continue feeling His love so powerfully.

There are certainly times when I don't feel His love. Thankfully, one of the great comforts of the Old Testament is the continual, repeated, incessant assertion by God that no matter how often we do things that remove ourselves from the ability to feel His love, He will *always* love us. Through His prophet Isaiah He promises us, "For the mountains might depart, and the hills may be removed, but my loving kindness shall not depart from thee, neither shall the covenant of my peace be removed, saith the Lord that hath mercy on thee" (Isa. 54:10, author's translation). Isaiah is teaching us that we would be mistaken to say that God's love for us is as stable and immovable as the great mountains of the world, because it is *more* stable and immovable! Nothing will cause Him to stop loving us—*nothing*! This is one of the most oft-repeated messages of the scriptures, particularly of the Old Testament.

God's Love in the Old Testament

It is crucial that we understand the scriptural assurances of God's love, especially in the Old Testament. One common idea suggests a God of justice in the Old Testament and a God of mercy in the New

Testament. I reject this notion. It results from a lackadaisical study of the Old Testament and a glossing-over of the New Testament. Those who do not see justice in the New Testament have forgotten accounts of the Savior cleansing the temple, unflinchingly berating the Pharisees, prophesying of the destruction of Jerusalem, and cursing the fig trees. They have also failed to notice some of the most touching scenes and sayings in the Old Testament—or have simply focused on only half of the story. They have seen Sodom destroyed without noticing God's willingness to spare it or His deliverance of Lot from destruction. They have read of Hagar being cast out of camp but missed God miraculously saving her in the desert, watching over her, and giving her and her son a powerful covenant. They remember that God slew the firstborn but forget that He offered a chance for everyone to avoid this tragedy. They have thought about Miriam being struck by leprosy but have not pondered the meaning behind her healing.

Perhaps this pattern of partial perception should not be surprising. It is in our nature to see those things that seem different to us more than to notice those tender mercies we have come to expect from the Lord. The Old Testament is the most culturally different of all our scriptural texts, so we are apt to find more surprises there. The tendency is to focus on the surprises and overlook the Godly loving kindness that has become the norm in all of scriptures. How sad—even perilous—to miss poignant stories of God's mercy.

There is danger in thinking of the Old Testament as a story of justice and the New Testament as one of mercy. First, we fail to see that God is an unchanging and consistent God. Moreover, if we cannot see God's great love for us in the Old Testament, we are likely to either feel His love less than we are entitled to or to modify our understanding of the nature of God and the scriptures in order to reconcile our misunderstanding with what we are reading.

Historically the latter has happened in a way that led many deep into paths of apostasy. In early Christianity, a large group of people followed what is known as Gnostic Christianity. Part of Gnostic teachings was that the god of the Old Testament was not God at all, but some kind of an aberrant demigod who was full of wrath. According to that belief, the one true God, who was far removed from men, finally sent Christ to earth in order to fix the mess that had happened under the reign of this angry being.

I believe this incredibly incorrect doctrine arose from the perception that the God of the Old Testament was full of only wrath and justice. Finding themselves unable to reconcile such an idea with the knowledge that God is full of love, these early Christians must have felt the need to do something to "fix" their misaligned perception of deity. If they had understood all of scripture better, they would not have felt the need to invent a story to account for their misunderstanding of the God of the Old Testament.

If only they had understood, as President Kimball did, that "The image of a loving, forgiving God comes through clearly to those who read and understand the scriptures. Since He is our Father, He naturally desires to raise us up, not to push us down, to help us live, not to bring about our spiritual death."[1]

At times this issue can become confusing for Latter-day Saints, who know that the Jehovah of the Old Testament is the Jesus Christ of the New Testament—and who thus may be wondering if they are learning about the nature of God the Father as they read the Old Testament. This happens when we forget that Jesus Christ, as Jehovah, represents the Father to us. Through divine investiture of authority, He is acting for and in behalf of the Father, and thus speaks as if He actually *were* the Father. His role is ever to reveal the Father to us (see John 14:7–10), and we can best understand the loving nature of the Father in the Old Testament if we read that book and think of Jehovah as God the Father, even though we know that it is the Son acting in the Father's place. It is, after all, the Son doing only that which the Father would do (see John 5:19). Their characteristics and traits are indistinguishable.

Another issue that can make it difficult for us to see God's love in the Old Testament stems from its transmission process. While the Old Testament is an amazing and valuable book, and we should be grateful to those who have worked so hard to make it available to us (see 2 Ne. 29:4), it also passed through some hands that took out some of the most plain and precious parts (see 1 Ne. 13:28–29; A of F 8). As I read the Joseph Smith Translation of the Old Testament, especially those portions now available in the book of Moses, I see how prevalent the theme of God's love was and how much is now missing. Yet we are fortunate that so much of the message of God's love to us was encoded into the Old Testament in a way that it was impossible for it all to be taken out. God had His scriptural writers embed His most important messages—those about His love and deliverance—in the stories that traverse the sacred pages of the Old Testament. We struggle to find God's most important messages when we don't know the stories, or how to read the stories, or how to use the context of the stories to get more out of the prophetic passages. He has left the messages there— hidden just enough beneath the surface that they were not removed from the text, yet not so far that we cannot uncover them with a small effort. He has given us many tools to help in that effort.

The Joseph Smith Translation is one of these tools. While many have historically struggled to see the love of God in the Old Testament, as Latter-day Saints we have an advantage because we have portions of the Old Testament available to us that others do not. Think of the image portrayed of God in Enoch's great vision, restored to us by Joseph Smith. Enoch saw in vision one of the hallmarks of God's justice: the flood. The flood can be viewed as an act of wrath, a heavy-handed sword of justice falling upon a wicked world. Indeed, God Himself said, "My fierce anger is kindled against them" (Moses 7:34). But when Enoch saw the story of the flood in vision, he also saw God weeping. Enoch asked God how He, an all-powerful being, could weep. Can you see the love and tenderness in the Lord's reply? "Should not the heavens weep, seeing these shall suffer?" (Moses 7:37).

Think of what we learn of God in this brief exchange. Because of the wickedness of the people, God has to mete out justice. At the same time, He sees the suffering and misery of His children. He talks about them being the workmanship of His own hands, and their suffering causes Him such great sorrow that He weeps. He seems to be weeping both because of the misery they bring upon themselves due to their wickedness and because of the suffering they go through as He brings justice upon them. Here we get only a small glimpse of how intensely God feels about His children, even those He described as the most wicked of all His creations.

God allowed Enoch to feel something of the depth of those feelings. When Enoch beheld the misery of mankind, he "wept and stretched forth his arms, and his heart swelled wide as eternity; and his bowels yearned; and all eternity shook" (Moses 7:41). Can you imagine the profundity of feeling Enoch was experiencing? Surely God experienced even more. We are utterly incapable of understanding the depth of God's love for us but we must not let our incapacity make us ignorant of that love, even in the midst of God's justice.

Instead, let us remember that when we have messed up, even repeatedly, God still loves us and is ever waiting to pardon us. "Let the wicked forsake his way, and the unrighteous man his thoughts: and let him return unto the Lord, and he will have mercy upon him; and to our God, for he will abundantly pardon" (Isa. 55:7). What a comforting thought! Surely we are all in need of hearing this from our Divine Father, for every single one of us has gone astray. It is our tendency to look at the strengths of those around us and then to look at ourselves and see our abundant mistakes. Not one of us has been exempt from moments where we knew we had just done something wrong—again! Often it is the same wrong thing we have already promised we wouldn't ever do again. While this realization can bring heavy and dismal discouragement, it is not as powerful as what Isaiah said about God's desire to pardon us. No matter how ample our sins and mistakes, they are no match for God's mercy, for He "will abundantly pardon!"

Even those hyper-wicked souls who died in the flood were not removed from God's love. He loved them so much He continued to reach out to them in the next life, trying yet again to bring them back to Him. He was willing to abundantly pardon even them—and, millennia later, He has not given up on them.

The Parable of the Defiant Daughter, or Why We Need to Know God Loves Us

Another danger stems from not recognizing God's great love for us, and to me it is best illustrated by my daughter. I have a petite, blonde, blue-eyed three-year-old who is an amazing combination of sweetness and fiery independence. Like any child her age, she sometimes does things she needs to be taught are wrong. When I correct her, that fiery independence often leads her to turn and look at me with her tiny hands balled up and pressed against her hips, her face upturned to reveal a clenched jaw, her blue eyes blazing with defiance. I finally realized that she *will not* give in or learn from me when she feels this way. I have learned that if I kneel down and hold my arms open, she quickly runs to me and wraps her small arms around my neck. She gives me a kiss, tells me she is sorry, and vows not to repeat the misbehavior. Why the difference? When I show her I still love her, her sweetness kicks in and she is ready to learn.

I suspect we are all like my daughter to some degree. If we don't see and feel God's love for us, we are much less likely to learn from Him as He tries to chastise and correct us. Unless we learn to find God's love expressed in the scriptures, we are, even unconsciously, far more likely to find ourselves spiritually standing with our hands on our hips and our jaw clenched. The truth is that the Lord is kneeling down with His arms open, waiting for us to run to Him and feel His love. All we need to do is learn to see the signs in the scriptures that tell us He is waiting for us that way. The signs are there; we just need to find them. Not only will our lives be much more rich and full, we will learn all the better. We misunderstand what the Lord is really doing in our lives when we fail to see what His words teach us about His love.

As I visit with Latter-day Saints, I find that many of us concentrate so much on the things we have done wrong or on our character flaws and shortcomings that we prevent ourselves from feeling God's love. Too many know that God is a loving being but do not feel or believe that He loves us specifically. That belief is like a weight tied around our neck—it drags us down, holds us back, and makes every aspect of life more burdensome and less joyful.

Not knowing of God's love for you is a real and personal tragedy. It can be debilitating but is completely unnecessary. God loves each of us, regardless of whom we are or what we have done. We must come to recognize this. God has been trying to tell us, but too often we unconsciously put on blinders and avoid the evidence. Instead, we must learn to see God's love in all the places in which He has painted it for us. One of these places is His written word.

Correctly identifying God's love for us in the scriptures is more easily done when we remember God's real purpose, which is to bring us exalted joy. This is His purpose because He loves us. As Elder Jeffrey R. Holland taught, an obvious evidence of God's great love for us is the fact that He was willing to have the Savior—His completely righteous, totally obedient, absolutely sinless Son—suffer indescribable pain and agony as a sacrifice for all of us.[2]

Realizing that God loves us with an immovable love that is deeper than we can fathom, no matter what, changes everything. Elder John H. Groberg described the effect when He said that filled with God's love, we can see and do and comprehend and endure things we can't otherwise—much as the Savior was able to endure what He did through His love for us.[3]

The Old Testament as an Overarching Canvas of God's Love

It is important that we become thoroughly familiar with the scriptures in order to understand God's love. We cannot be familiar with just part of the scriptures, nor with what others say about the scriptures, nor possess only a brief understanding of the storyline of the scriptures. Any of those approaches may lead us to misunderstand this vital concept. If we *kind of* read the scriptures—enough to be familiar with stories where we see God's vengeance and justice—but do not take the time to think about what God says about these events, nor try to tie them back in with His primary purpose, we will misunderstand who God is and how He feels about us. If we read only the scriptures that contain portions we like, such as parts of the Book of Mormon and the Gospels, we will likewise misunderstand who God is and how He feels about us. Similarly, if we rely on commentators who have come to see differing divine personality traits in the Old and New Testaments, we will still misunderstand who God is and how He feels about us. Such a misunderstanding will inevitably lead us to feel alienated from God, and we cannot afford to entertain anything that leads us away from God.

Now that we have come to understand why it is so important to find and feel God's love, in particular why it is so important to experience it in the Old Testament, we must learn how to read that sacred book in a manner that makes this possible. Let's journey through a few themes and passages that will better equip us to understand symbols, stories, and sayings in our oldest book of scripture. Through this exercise, you'll emerge with a perspective that allows you to see the sweeping vista of God's overwhelming mercy and compassion for His children. You should then be able to read the Old Testament in such a way that its pages will open and reveal a vibrant tapestry of the Lord's love for you and the potential He sees in you.

Not only will we delve into significant Old Testament symbols that are used to convey these crucial messages, but we will also frequently follow an ancient symbol with a matching modern symbol, parable, parallel, or analogy. Because so much of the Old Testament speaks through symbols or symbolic stories, and because sometimes those symbols are difficult for us to understand, I have found it helpful to use these modern-day parallels in conjunction with Biblical symbols. Such a technique not only explains the symbol, but typically helps students of the Old Testament gain the ability to decipher other ancient Biblical symbols on their own. It equips them to read the stories in which God embedded so many of His messages for us.

This technique of combining ancient symbols and symbolic actions with modern ones should help us gain a few skills and perspectives that will serve like a key to a locked box. When we know what to look for and how to look at it, we will find Old Testament passages opening up and revealing a loving-kindness in which we can revel. This unlocked perspective will sweep us up and carry us closer to the Lord.

The *Lectures on Faith* teach us that in order to receive salvation we must have a correct idea of God's attributes and characteristics. Primary among these characteristics is God's love for us. Similarly, we *must* be able to see in all of scripture what Elder Neal A. Maxwell taught us about God—that, as a God of love, His plan of salvation represents not only mercy and power, but His relentless, redeeming love. Though He denounces sin and hates our vices, He loves *us* with an enormous, perfect love.[4]

The theme of God's love for us and His desire to help us return to Him is really the essence of the gospel. This idea pervades the Old Testament and is interwoven in other books of scripture, for the Old Testament carries the same gospel message that the rest of God's scriptures do. While that message is consistently conveyed throughout the standard works, its broadest brush strokes are painted in our oldest scriptural record. The Old Testament provides a large-scale canvas on which God has painted in rich color and varied textures the picture of His love for us.

While we will never be able to fully fathom the depth and strength of God's love for us in this life, the closer we approach that understanding the more joy, satisfaction, comfort, and security we will experience. We will feel it seeping deep within us, permeating every thought and feeling we have. It will fill up everything we see around us, causing us to live life on a different plane and to enjoy life more abundantly. We cannot let anything—especially our own sins—rob us of this understanding.

Consider what God told Israel through His prophet Malachi. By Malachi's day, Israel had been blessed so abundantly, had then sinned so greatly, had been delivered time and again by the Lord, and were yet inexorably creeping back into sin. In fact, they were on the very door of apostasy. Though the children of Israel were once again turning their backs on the Lord after He had helped them so much, God told them, "I have loved you, Saith the Lord" (Mal. 1:2). Read this as if the Lord were speaking directly to you. Whatever your relationship with God has been, He wants you to know He loves you. Furthermore, the Lord went on through Malachi to tell Israel (and us), "**Return** unto me and I will **return** unto you" (Mal. 3:7; emphasis added). In other words, no matter how you have messed up, despite your frailties, in the face of your rebelliousness, and through all your shortcomings, God has loved you and always will. He is always trying to help you return to Him. Together we will see how the idea of a loving God helping us **return** to Him is one of the overarching themes of the Old Testament. The breathtaking, exhilarating, suffusing panorama of God's love awaits us.

CHAPTER TWO
A PLAN, A COVENANT, AND CORRECTION INSPIRED BY LOVE

Now when I passed by thee, and looked upon thee, behold,
thy time was the time of love; and I spread my wing over thee, and cov-
ered thy nakedness: yea, I sware unto thee,
and entered into a covenant with thee,
saith the Lord GOD, and you became mine.
(Ezek. 16:8, author's translation)

Whom I love I also chasten that their sins may be forgiven,
for with the chastisement I prepare a way for their deliverance
in all things out of temptation, and I have loved you—
(D&C 95:1)

Being Bound by Love

BECAUSE THE LORD LOVES US so much, He is willing to establish a covenant with us. He is willing to bind us to Him both because He wants us to be exalted and because *only He* has the power to exalt us. Thus, He ties us to Himself, allowing us to draw on His exalting power. Once we have covenanted with God we have left neutral ground forever. When we have become part of the covenant, He will never, ever leave us alone again. He will always push us toward our exaltation, no matter how often we may try to go a different way. The problem is, sometimes we don't like the way He pushes us.

In order to fully understand how God works with us inside a covenant relationship, we have to learn to read the scriptures in a particular way. We have to realize that what God does with His covenant people as a whole is the same thing He does with you and me individually as a covenant person. In the same way the Lord works with Israel as a whole, so He works with you as an Israelite individual (keeping in mind that anyone who has entered into a covenant with God has become part of the house of Israel). This realization allows us to take what God does with and teaches ancient Israel and apply it to ourselves. Since the most sweeping stories involving Israel are in the Old Testament, seeing ourselves in Israel will cause us to be caught up in epic events. We will start to view the stories and characters as being about us. Suddenly we will see the Old Testament promises to Israel in a whole new light—a light that bathes us in the brilliance of God's love for us.

For example, when we feel as if we are becoming enslaved to sin, bad choices, bad circumstances, or bad whatever, we would do well to remember what God said to Israel. "Because the Lord loved you, and because he would keep the oath which he had sworn unto your fathers, hath the Lord brought you out with a mighty hand, and redeemed you out of the house of bondmen" (Deut. 7:8). Clearly God will deliver you both because of His love and to honor the covenant He has made with you. He made the covenant because He loves you: "The Lord had a delight in thy fathers to love them, and he chose their seed after them, even you above all people" (Deut. 10:15). To compound this, because we have made a covenant with God, He is bound to love us all the more: "The Lord thy God shall keep unto thee the covenant and the mercy which he sware unto thy fathers: And he will love thee, and bless thee, and multiply thee" (Deut. 7:12–13).

What Covenantal Love Means

The Old Testament teaches about a special kind of love, mercy, and kindness available only within the context of a covenant. While God loves all His children, those who have entered into a covenant with Him will find extra access to patience and mercy. In our Bible, the word for this is most often translated as *kindness, loving kindness,* or *mercy*. Because of translation issues, it is not always easy to identify when the Lord is speaking about this special covenantal love. But despite those translation difficulties, the Old Testament is clear that God will continuously extend mercy and forgiveness to those who have been willing to covenant with Him.

Let's learn some lessons from the Old Testament about how God's covenantal love works—about how God will work with you as a covenant holder because He loves you so much. Again, we must take the case of Israel as a whole and apply it to ourselves as Israelite individuals. As we do this, we will see that despite how poorly we often act—even how repeatedly we act poorly—we will not move beyond either God's ability or His desire to work with us, because His is a desire and ability born of love. I am not espousing that we quit trying to do better; I *am* highlighting the idea that our ability to mess up is not stronger than God's love for us.

This is amply illustrated when we see how much Israel messed up. After God had delivered them, set them up in a promised land, helped them conquer their enemies, and helped them become mighty kingdoms, they still fell into great iniquity. We cannot possibly enumerate all of Israel's sins here, but one verse from Jeremiah gives us a glimpse as to how wicked they had really become: "They have forsaken me, and have estranged this place [the temple], and have burned incense in it unto other gods, whom neither they nor their fathers have known, nor the kings of Judah, and have filled this place with the blood of innocents; They have built also the high places of Baal, to burn their sons with fire for burnt offerings unto Baal" (Jer. 19:4–5).

Few of us will ever come close to matching this level of wickedness: desecrating the temple, shedding the blood of innocents, or sacrificing children to false gods. Moreover, the Israelites were following false prophets, persecuting and trying to kill the true prophets, and simultaneously oppressing the poor, the orphans, and the widows. This was a depraved people.

As a result of their wickedness, the Lord came out in justice against them, and they were conquered and carried off captive. It is tempting to think of this as an act of the wrath of God, and to some degree it can be seen in this light. But looking at the larger picture, we can see that while justice was served, the Lord was also full of love and compassion. Remember the glimpse of God's feelings that Enoch afforded us when the Lord had to send the flood? "Wherefore, should not the heavens weep seeing these shall suffer?" (Moses 7:37). It seems it pained God to see the suffering that His children brought upon themselves. Perhaps we are best afforded a chance to see why God punishes the wicked in the Old Testament.

When enumerating Israel's wickedness, the Lord asks Ezekiel, "Have I any pleasure at all that the wicked should die? saith the Lord GOD: and not that he should **return** from his ways, and live?" (Ezek. 18:23; emphasis added). The Lord answers His own question in two ways. He first tells Ezekiel, "when the wicked man **turneth** away from his wickedness that he hath committed, and doeth that which is lawful and right, he shall save his soul alive" (Ezek. 18:27; emphasis added). And then more specifically He says, "For I have no pleasure in the death of him that dieth, saith the Lord God: wherefore **turn** yourselves, and live ye" (Ezek. 18:32; emphasis added). The Lord is telling us that He does not want for us to reap the inevitable consequence of sin. What He wants is for us to change, to **turn** away from wickedness, and to receive His greatest blessings. We will return to these verses many times, as they color so many things that the Lord tells His people.

He Knew We Would Mess Up

When we understand that the plan of salvation was born of love, we more fully understand every part of that plan, including our own little role in it. The whole reason God created the plan was because He loves us so much that He wants to make more of us than we have ever considered making of ourselves. Every aspect of the plan, every element of the scriptures describing the plan, every feature of the Restoration is an expression of God's love for us. There are no commandments, no Church programs, and no guidelines that are born out of a desire to restrict but rather out of a will to exalt. Truly, "He doeth not anything save it be for the benefit of the world; for he loveth the world" (2 Ne. 26:24).

Surely when God created the plan of salvation He knew we would mess up. He knew before we were even part of the plan that we would sometimes fail spectacularly. This was all incorporated into the plan, as anyone who understands the role of the Savior realizes. Even so, we often struggle with the idea that we do mess up. Or perhaps it is better stated that we do not struggle with the idea—we usually get the concept—but with the reality that we have yet again done things the wrong way. The struggle to feel God's love often comes when our intentions and behavior are not as good as we know they should be or as good as we want them to be. Yet this should not be the case. God expected we would be thus, and He incorporated it into His plan.

I am not advocating that since God knew we would fall short, we might as well stop trying to do better. Instead I am suggesting that as we try to do better we should not be surprised that frequently we don't. Nor should we let that keep us from coming to God and partaking of His love.

An experience I had with my son can help us understand several Biblical passages. I loved riding my bike when I was a kid, and as a parent I looked forward to teaching my children this liberating skill. But as I set out to teach my first child, I found that teaching was much harder than I had anticipated. Naturally, I understood that it takes a while to get the feel for keeping your balance, and in theory I expected that. What I didn't expect was that each time I let go of the back of my son's bike I could see what he was doing wrong—and that his fear often led to his failure to ride the way I had taught him. This frustrated me, and initially I was not very good at dealing with his failures. I knew that if he just did things the way I told him, he would be able to ride the bike—but his fear inhibited his learning. I was not happy about it.

After taking a small break and thinking about our situation, I realized how ridiculous I was being. Of course children are nervous when they learn to ride a bike. Of course they won't do things right at first, even if they have been instructed properly. They have to lean too far one way and too far the other in order to learn how to keep their balance. But leaning too far can be frightening, so they give up. I decided to try to do better, to express more confidence and approval in the learning process.

When we started again, my son got nervous and stopped, just as he had before. He looked at me, ready for disapproval and disappointment. Fortunately I had progressed a little, and no longer expected him to learn without first failing to do what I had taught him. Eventually he did learn, and now, years later, it's difficult to get him *off* his bike!

I wonder how many of us fear that the Lord will be disappointed as we learn our way through life. But we don't have imperfect mortal examples, the kind of example I was to my son as he learned to ride his bike; instead, we have a perfect and loving Father. He knows that we won't learn without falling a few times. He knows that despite giving us perfect instructions, sometimes we will just fail to follow them—and then we will fall off. This is part of learning. For one reason or another, we lose our balance or become afraid, and we just don't follow His instructions. Our loving Father knew it would work this way.

As already noted, it is because He knew we would continually fall short that God sent His Son, our Savior. The atoning sacrifice of the Redeemer was a result of both God's and Christ's love for us, stemming from a deeply held desire to make us whole after we wound ourselves. As Elder Russell M. Nelson noted, Jesus suffered as deeply as He did because He loves us deeply—and He wants us to repent so He can fully heal us.[5] As Isaiah teaches, Christ was wounded with our transgressions so that He could bring us peace and healing (see Isa. 53:5).

Yet so often when we have messed up—again!—we flee from the peace that He stands ready to offer us. This happens when we don't realize how willing the Lord is to continually forgive us. One of His oft-repeated attributes is His longsuffering. For example, He is described as "merciful and gracious, longsuffering, and abundant in goodness and truth" (Ex. 34:6). He is praised thus: "The Lord is longsuffering, and of great mercy, forgiving iniquity and transgression" (Num. 14:18). He is "a God full of compassion, and gracious, longsuffering, and plenteous in mercy and truth" (Ps. 86:15). Because of His loving kindness and longsuffering toward us (see 1 Ne. 19:9), He wants to forgive us *as often* as we are willing to repent (see Ezek. 18; Mosiah 26:30; Moro. 6:8). Still we somehow allow Satan to fool us into thinking that we have done the same thing wrong so many times that the Lord does not want to hear from us anymore about that issue or transgression. This is an outright lie; it flies in the face of the Lord's promise to forgive us *as often* as we repent.

Some of our penchant for believing Satan's lie stems from misunderstanding God's relationship with justice. This wrong impression can be created by the sweeping stories of the Old and New Testaments as well as the Book of Mormon. In both the Old Testament and Book of Mormon we see repeated patterns of a covenant people who become wicked and reap destruction as a result. The Old Testament story really continues in the New Testament, when Israel once again receives warning that their wickedness will bring destruction. Though John the Baptist, the Savior, and the apostles all warned of this, Israel rejected their teachings. The destruction of Jerusalem and so many other Jewish cities at the hand of the Romans was some of the greatest devastation the Israelites ever suffered. In some ways they are still in the process of recovering from that horrific destruction about which the Savior Himself had warned.

These panoramic stories of judgment can make us feel that repeated sin brings only justice. This is again a result of focusing on the judgment but forgetting that God then reached out to His people yet again. In fact, it is God's need to satisfy justice *coupled with* His desire to extend mercy that led to the creation of the plan of salvation and the gift of His Beloved Son. We do not fully understand God's love unless we understand justice. As President Boyd K. Packer taught, it is justice that invokes the Atonement and allows us to fully put Satan behind us, because our debt has been paid in full by the Savior, the only perfect person who ever lived.[6]

A Loving Escape

One of the reasons I don't see a God full of vengeance and wrath in the Old Testament is because within that book I see so many times when the Lord goes out of His way to help His people escape punishment. One of the principle themes of the Old Testament is that of substitution. Let's look at just a few examples.

In Egypt, every firstborn was to die as part of the plagues. However, the Lord allowed the Israelites a substitute: If they would slay a firstborn, unblemished lamb, the shedding of that blood would stand as a proxy for the firstborn of that family (see Ex. 12) and the firstborn child would be spared. In this they must surely have been reminded of Isaac being spared from sacrifice as the Lord provided a ram to serve as his substitute (see Gen. 22).

The Lord then asked the Israelites to repay Him by dedicating their firstborn to Him. But again a substitute was arranged. Instead of each family giving up its firstborn, Israel as a whole gave one of Israel's children as a substitute. Hence the tribe of Levi became the family dedicated to serving the Lord, serving as a substitute for the oldest male in each family (see Num. 3:12; 8:9–18).

Many of the sacrifices carried out under the law of Moses used an animal as a substitute for an Israelite. In these cases, the errant Israelite would place his hands on the head of the animal and symbolically transfer sins and trespasses to the animal, who then stood as a substitute for the Israelite as it paid the price of sin: death. In this way the Lord taught how much He wanted to save Israel from her just punishments by providing a substitute.

Nowhere is this more clear than in the most sacred day and festival of the law of Moses. One of the culminating elements of the Day of Atonement (Yom Kippur) was when the high priest placed his hands on a goat, pronounced the sins of all Israel upon it, and drove it out of the camp (see Lev. 16). Tradition holds that the goat was driven off a cliff to ensure that it never came back to camp. The goat served as a substitute for all of Israel, taking the punishment of their sins upon it so that they did not have pay the price themselves.

Under the law of Moses, if a person could not repay a debt, he had to sell his lands, his family, or even himself into slavery in order to make as much of a payment as possible. But the Lord again provided for a substitute payment. The closest kinsman was supposed to serve as a redeemer. He was to pay the unmet price, thus nullifying the punishment that his poorer kinsman had not been able to avoid. This was one of the reasons the birthright child received a double inheritance—he was to substitute for any family members who could not pay their debts. This is the imagery that the phrase "Redeemer of Israel" draws on. In this case the payment or punishment still had to be met, but the redeemer would step in and take the payment upon himself (see Lev. 25).

There are countless other examples. In each the symbolism is designed to teach us what the Lord does for Israel as a whole and how it relates to what He will do for each one of us. In each the substitution helps us understand how the Savior willingly makes Himself a substitute for us, taking the punishment upon Himself so we don't have to (see D&C 19). How could we more clearly see that God does not find joy in punishing us?

There's another point as well: The Atonement makes it abundantly clear that the Lord is more than willing to help us escape punishment.

Yet there are times when it is best for us not to have a substitute. In many situations a loving God does not deflect a punishment (or other kinds of difficulties) because that trying time is exactly what we need. While the concept of substitution should convince us that God does not delight in punishing us, it also highlights that there must be times when, despite His desire to provide a substitute, it is better for us to feel some measure of His wrath. His great love for us forces Him to sometimes inflict just the right kind of chastisement.

Punishment with a Purpose

If we do not understand God's plan for us—and especially how that plan and God's love dictate the way He will work with us—we will certainly misunderstand the messages portrayed by the large-scale, epic story of Israel in our scriptures. As noted above, it can become easy for us to focus on the repeated pattern of judgment and destruction that we see in the Book of Mormon and the Old Testament. The same pattern is also hinted at in the New Testament, though the actual destruction of Jerusalem that is part of the New Testament story was not recorded in scriptures. One could ask how the Savior could speak of turning the other cheek but also warn of a quick and violent destruction of Jerusalem that seems to be part of God's justice (see Matt. 24). We could wonder how a God who speaks of healing His people could allow the Nephites to be completely destroyed (see Morm. 9). We could question a God who speaks of an unending mercy but also allows Assyrians and Babylonians to overrun His covenant people in their promised land (see 2 Kgs. 17 and 2 Kgs. 25). These questions arise from seeing part of the story—the judgment part—but not noticing how God reaches out to His people afterward. There is always an *afterward* because it is the next natural step after the loving but firm punishment that God has to deliver to His chosen people.

I believe the Old Testament book of Hosea illustrates better than any other portion of scripture how God works with an astray covenant people—or an astray covenant person. The message is carried partially by what Hosea says but more so by what God asks him to do. Whatever the personal circumstances of Hosea's life turned out to be, the book tells us a story that is intended to be applied symbolically to Israel as a whole and to each Israelite individual.

Hosea is told to marry a harlot named Gomer. In this, Hosea represents the Lord and Gomer represents all of Israel and each Israelite not faithful in his or her covenants with God (see Hosea 1). After years of marriage and the birth of children, Gomer was still seemingly playing the harlot, seeking for the payment of corn, wine, oil, bread, flax, wool, figs, and vines from her various lovers (see Hosea 2:5). The Lord tells Hosea that He plans to take away all of these good things, destroy her vines and fig trees, bring in wild animals to eat up her food, turn her beautiful and fruitful plants into thorns, and take away even her happiness (see Hosea 2:5–6, 11).

While this may not sound like a very kind thing to do, the Lord tells us why He is doing it: "And she shall follow after her lovers, but she shall not overtake them; and she shall seek them, but shall not find them: then shall she say, I will go and return to my first husband; for then was it better with me than now. For she did not know that I gave her corn, and wine, and oil, and multiplied her silver and gold" (Hosea 2:7–8). God did not take away the wine, corn, and other payments just for the sake of justice. He did it so that Gomer/Israel would return to her true husband.

The meaning of this story is profound, its impact life-changing. Here we learn something of how the Lord operates. He is not punishing Gomer just because she has done wrong. He is punishing her in such a way that she will **return** to Hosea. God also makes it very clear that He is doing the same thing with Israel. All of the wrath or justice of God we hear about in the book of Hosea—and there is plenty, as this was the last warning the kingdom of Israel received before being destroyed—is aimed at leading Israel to realize they need to **return** to God.

The metaphor of taking away Gomer's payments and pleasures is so meaningful. Gomer was playing the harlot because she wanted the payment. When that payment (or the pleasure that came from the payment) was taken away, she realized that there was no point in playing the harlot. She also recognized she had been taken care of by Hosea all along; she didn't ever need to play the harlot to receive corn and oil. Gomer **returned** to her husband because life was better for her when she was with him. This is exactly what the Lord is trying to do with Israel.

As I describe what the Lord is doing for Israel, ask yourself if this matches anything that ever happens in your life: The Lord takes care of Israel but still they stray and wander. Thus the Lord metes out inevitable justice in a way that helps Israel realize they are not finding what they sought for when they strayed from God. In fact, they will realize that only in serving God and remaining faithful would they find what they really want and need.

This was not a one-time effort on the part of the Lord. Israel messed up again and again, and justice came each time. Note what the Lord says to Hosea about Israel: "Though I have bound and strengthened their arms, yet do they imagine mischief against me" (Hosea 7:15). We are often surprised that after all the Lord had done for them, Israel still turned against Him. Yet most of us know we are often as guilty as was Israel, despite all the Lord has done for us. This is why it is so comforting to realize that the Lord will continue to work with Israel, because it teaches us that He will also continue to work with us.

This is made abundantly clear at the end of chapter five and the beginning of chapter six of Hosea. The Lord says, "I will be unto Ephraim as a lion, and as a young lion to the house of Judah: I, even I, will tear and go away; I will take away and none shall rescue him" (Hosea 5:14). This is a terrifying image of the wrath of God. Because Ephraim has been blessed so much (as we have been) and yet still turns away (as each of us sometimes does), the Lord will rip him up like a lion rips up its prey. Think of that image applied to your life. Think of havoc being wrought in all you do with no rescue, no one else strong enough to pull you away from your deserved judgment.

Such an image is frightening but it is immediately followed by an explanation as to why the Lord does this: "I will go and return to my place, till they acknowledge their offence, and seek my face: in their affliction they will seek me early" (Hosea 5:15). It turns out that the Lord will bring vengeance upon Israel (in the destruction of the kingdom of Israel and the scattering of the Ten Tribes), and then abandon them (as they began to wander). He doesn't do this out of a desire for revenge, nor is it a response to any capricious emotion. He does it because He knows that when Israel is afflicted they will seek Him again, just as Gomer would return to Hosea when she found no profit in playing the harlot.

The success of the Lord's efforts is confirmed in the next two verses. Put yourself in the place of the Ephraimites as they say, "Come, and let us **return** unto the Lord: for he hath torn, and he will heal us; he hath smitten, and he will bind us up. After two days will he revive us: in the third day he will raise us up, and we shall live in his sight" (Hosea 6:1–2; emphasis added). The certainty expressed here is reassuring. Though Ephraim has sinned repeatedly and has been smitten and torn by the Lord as a result, Ephraimites are still sure that God is waiting—willing to heal them, to bind up their wounds, to raise them up so they can live with Him.

Note the beautiful language God uses as He describes His constant willingness to forgive Israel by comparing Israel to Hosea and Gomer. Speaking of the time Gomer would decide to return, God says, "And it shall be at that day, saith the Lord, that thou shalt call me *Ishi*; and shalt call me no more *Baali*" (Hosea 2:16; emphasis added).

The beauty of this statement is understood better with some vocabulary explanation. Two words are most often used to denote someone as a husband in Hebrew. *Baali* means "my husband" but has connotations of "my lord/master husband." *Ish* (pronounced eesh) literally means "man" but also means "husband" in a more endearing sense, so *Ishi* means "my man/husband." What the Lord is saying here is that before we may have had a less close relationship, and when we return we can have a relationship full of a great deal more love—our relationship will be less like that between a servant woman and her master and more like a husband and wife. Of course, this is only possible if our return consists of such real repentance that the Atonement is able to change us—to change who we are. We'll discuss this is greater detail later.

In order to solidify in our minds the beauty of the relationship the Lord wants to have with us after we return, He continues using the metaphor of Hosea's marriage to Gomer, comparing it to His relationship with Israel or to you and me as Israelite individuals: "I will betroth thee unto me in righteousness, and in judgment, and in lovingkindness, and in mercies. I will betroth thee unto me in faithfulness: and thou shalt know the Lord" (Hosea 2:19–20). Here the touching, affectionate relationship of a sweet betrothal is underscored by the repeated use of words like *love*, *kindness*, and *mercy*.

Such is the tender and loving communion God is trying to establish with us despite how badly we may have messed up in the past.

As if this imagery were not enough, the Lord continues, seemingly very concerned with helping us see how much He wants us to return and how wonderful it will be when we do. Speaking of Gomer's/our return, He says, "And it shall come to pass in that day, I will hear, saith the Lord, I will hear the heavens, and they shall hear the earth; and the earth shall hear the corn, and the wine, and the oil; and they shall hear Jezreel [a fertile valley]. And I will sow her unto me in the earth; and I will have mercy upon her that had not obtained mercy; and I will say to them which were not my people, Thou art my people; and they shall say, Thou art my God" (Hosea 2:21–23). We, like Israel—who had abandoned God and ceased being a covenant people—can return to God, renew our covenant, and once again be His people. Seemingly to emphasize His point, the Lord has become redundant as He again tells Israel that it does not matter how big or small the mess we have made is, nor how often we have sinned or forgotten our promises to God. Regardless of any of that, He is waiting to once again number us among "His people."

In the end, the Lord was assured of success with Israel. He knew that "Ephraim shall say, What have I to do any more with idols?" (Hosea 14:8). And once they said this, He promised He would "heal their backsliding, I will love them freely: for mine anger is turned away from him. I will be as the dew unto Israel" (Hosea 14:4–5).

As the Lord speaks of His love again and again, can you feel how emphatic He is? By the sheer volume of His repeated reminders of His unending love, the Lord assures us that if we will continue to try to come back to Him—as Ephraim did and has been doing for millennia—the Lord will heal us and love us freely.

Such is the stirring message of Hosea, a theme that undergirds the entire Old Testament. Israel, Gomer, you, and I will repeatedly mess up. Thus we will surely be punished. But the punishment is not capricious; it is punishment with a purpose. It is punishment aimed specifically at bringing us back to the Lord. It is the Lord, in loving kindness and mercy, reaching out to us, guiding us, healing us, and loving us freely. This is the God of the Old Testament, New

Testament, and all eternity, reaching out to His children in great mercy, using any number of means to bring us back into His loving arms.

CHAPTER THREE
PUSHING US TO RETURN TO HIM

Behold, happy is the man whom God correcteth:
therefore despise not the chastening
of the Almighty.
(Job 5:17)

My son, despise not the chastening of the Lord,
neither be weary of his correction.
(Prov. 3:11)

Jeremiah's Additional Witness

WHILE THE BOOK OF HOSEA typifies the Lord's desire and method of bringing us back to Him, it is not the only place in the Old Testament where God teaches His people—teaches us—why He is punishing them. As the kingdom of Judah neared destruction at the hands of Babylon, Jeremiah strenuously tried to get his people to repent. Despite tremendous persecution and opposition, he hoped Israel would turn from their wicked ways and avoid their pending doom. Listen to Jeremiah and the Lord as they try to explain to Israel how they are working with them: "For I am with thee, saith the Lord, to save thee: though I make a full end of all nations whither I have scattered thee, yet will I not make a full end of thee: but I will correct thee in measure, and will not leave thee altogether unpunished" (Jer. 30:11).

Though the Lord clearly hoped that His punishments would save Israel, this would not be the case for some time. Israel refused to let the Lord's chastisement force them to return to Him until it had become unbearable. Jeremiah was quick to notice Israel's failure to respond to the Lord's corrective measures. Early in his ministry he lamented that they had not responded to the Lord: "In vain have I smitten your children; they received no correction" (Jer. 2:30). Shortly afterward, Jeremiah acknowledged this problem again when he said to the Lord, "Thou hast stricken them, but they have not grieved; thou hast consumed them, *but* they have refused to receive correction: they have made their faces harder than a rock; they have refused to **return**" (Jer. 5:3; emphasis added). He also complained that "this is a nation that obeyeth not the voice of the Lord their God, nor receiveth correction" (Jer. 7:28). While in Israel's case it did not work that time, it is clear that Jeremiah understood why the Lord was striking His people and why He was punishing them: He wanted to correct them and get them to **return** to God.

It would be easy to read these verses and concentrate only on the fact that God was striking and consuming His people. We have to stop and think about it in order to realize that Jeremiah is telling us *why* God was doing so. This is true of Jeremiah's overall mission and message. For example, when we read "Is not my word like as a fire? saith the Lord and like a hammer that breaketh the rock in pieces?" (Jer. 23:29), we are apt to see God as a destructive being. But His pronouncements of hammering and breaking are seen in a different light when we look at Jeremiah's mission as a whole. At the very beginning of his book, Jeremiah records his commission from the Lord. The Lord spoke to Jeremiah, saying, "See, I have this day set thee over the nations and over the kingdoms, to root out, and to pull down, and to destroy, and to throw down, to build, and to plant" (Jer. 1:10). The verbs that stand out to us are *pulling down, destroying,* and *throwing down.* But the last two verbs give the entire statement meaning: Jeremiah is then to *build,* to *plant.* To me, the commission could be restated thus: "This people need to change—they need to start over. In order to get them to grow properly, you will have to destroy them so they can be built up the right way."

God and Jeremiah use agricultural metaphors as is so often done in the Old Testament. Even though our society is not nearly as agriculturally based as was ancient Israel's, I believe we can all understand the imagery employed. If we have some kind of tree or plant that has gone bad, that has become diseased or overcome by pests, often the only answer is to tear it down. If an area has become infested with a tenacious weed, typically the only remedy is to tear the whole thing out and start over. This is what the Lord is telling Jeremiah to do with his people. They have to be pulled up by the roots, to be torn down and destroyed. When that task has been accomplished, Jeremiah is to start over—to plant.

A building metaphor is also used. In our day we can relate to this symbol. We live in a day when a building deemed unsafe is torn down so that a new, better building can be built the right way in its place. This is why Jeremiah is told not only to throw down and to destroy but also to build. The dual metaphor in Jeremiah's commission sets the tone for his entire book. Because Israel had become so wicked, the Lord was about to bring upon them many great punishments. The purpose of those punishments, however, was not just to break them in pieces as vengeance for their repeated failure to follow the Lord. It was designed to bring them to a point where they could start over, where they would turn to the Lord and do things the right way. Their impending destruction was aimed at making Israel a people that the Lord could bring up in the right way, that were humble enough they would rely on the Lord and truly become His people.

Jeremiah understood that these principles were not only for Israel as a whole, but that they applied to him as an individual. He said to the Lord, "I know that the way of man is not in himself: it is not in man that walketh to direct His steps. O Lord, correct me, but with judgment; not in thine anger, lest thou bring me to nothing" (Jer. 10:23–24). Jeremiah understood his own need for correction and also hoped that he would accept that correction quickly so that the punishments would not have to be so severe. What a wise example for us to follow.

Ezekiel Agrees

Ezekiel also speaks on behalf of the Lord when he tells Israel that God is punishing them for a reason. As we read earlier, the Lord asked Ezekiel, "Have I any pleasure at all that the wicked should die? saith the Lord God: and not that he should **return** from his ways, and live?" (Ezek. 18:23; emphasis added). Clearly the Lord would rather not punish Israel. He would much rather they repent and come unto Him so that He might bless them. While the terrible things that befell the Jews were certainly a punishment for their sins, it was not fully due to justice. As in Hosea, through Ezekiel the Lord tells Israel why He punishes them. In Ezekiel 33 the Lord outlines the things the Jews had done wrong, including working abominations, defiling others' wives, worshiping idols, and shedding blood. As a result we read, "For I will lay the land most desolate, and the pomp of her strength shall cease; and the mountains of Israel shall be desolate, that none shall pass through" (Ezek. 33:28).

Clearly judgment is coming as the inevitable result of Israel's sins. Then the Lord explains why: "Then shall they know that I am the Lord, when I have laid the land most desolate because of all their abominations which they have committed. Also, thou son of man, the children of thy people still are talking against thee by the walls and in the doors of the houses, and speak one to another, every one to his brother, saying, Come, I pray you, and hear what is the word that cometh forth from the Lord" (Ezek. 33:29–30).

We see here that part of the purpose of the punishment was to convince Israel that the Lord was in command so they would actually listen to His word. The Lord was trying to guide them back to Him. So it is with us. As covenant partners with God, when we break that covenant, He will direct things into our lives that are designed to help us want to come back to Him, to listen to the "word that cometh forth from thy Lord." As with the Lord's determination to save Israel, all His efforts are aimed at helping us turn to Him again, for He has no pleasure in our punishment. He loves us; His desires are to help us **return** to Him.

I wish to be clear, for there is danger of being misunderstood here. Justice must come because it is an eternal principle. It is not administered capriciously or at random; it always accompanies sin. What we need to understand is that the Lord administers justice in a manner designed to evoke change. He metes out justice both because justice is necessary and because He uses it to nudge—or sometimes drive—us back to Him. Justice comes the way it does because God loves us. The Lord so often highlights this point throughout the Old Testament that a modern-day English teacher would excise much of the book in an effort to avoid redundancy. However, the Lord works differently. He uses repetition to teach, to emphasize, and to remind His children, who are wont to forget so easily.

Even after all His repeated messages to Israel, they still often missed the point. But by bringing the message before Israel again and again, the Lord will eventually succeed. The incessant repetition will eventually bring Israel back to their Father. We would do well to allow the Lord to bombard us with this repeated message. Absorbing such repetition will help us to more fully understand it and to have it more completely distill upon our souls. The Lord is emphatically clear. Justice comes, but due to God's compelling love for us, it does so in such a way that it pushes us to try again. Summed up, "Whom the Lord loveth, He correcteth" (Prov. 3:12).

We must not be afraid of that correction when it comes. When life's difficulties come upon us, or when we fail again, we can either choose to give up or choose to look for how the situation can help us become better. The Bible warns against dealing with the Lord's correction in the wrong way: "Correction is grievous unto him that forsaketh the way: and he that hateth reproof shall die" (Prov. 15:10). On the other hand, when we think of ourselves as His children, we see that the Lord hopes His correction will lead us toward Him and bring us peace: "correct thy son, and he shall give thee rest; yea, he shall give delight unto thy soul" (Prov. 29:17).

The Example of Job

Job is a premiere example of someone who took correction from the Lord and became a better person as a result. As Job and his friends spoke of the nature of God, God Himself gave them a reminder of who they were actually talking about. Out of a whirlwind, God pointedly asked Job, "Gird up now thy loins like a man; for I will demand of thee, and answer thou me. Where wast thou when I laid the foundations of the earth? Declare, if thou hast understanding. Who hast laid the measures thereof, if thou knowest? Or who hath stretched the line upon it? Whereupon are the foundations thereof fastened? Or who laid the corner stone thereof; When the morning stars sang together, and all the sons of God shouted for joy? . . . Hast thou commanded the morning since thy days; and caused the dayspring to know his place?" (Job 38:3–12).

The Lord asked Job such questions for seventy-two verses. Can you imagine being challenged in such a way by God Himself? Job immediately began to repent, telling the Lord, "Behold, I am vile, what shall I answer thee?" (Job 40:4). The Lord chastised Job in a similar manner for fifty-two more verses.

Finally Job answered, "I know that thou canst do everything, and that no thought can be witholden from thee. . . . I uttered that I understood not; things too wonderful for me, which I knew not. . . . I have heard of thee by hearing of the ear: but now mine eye seeth thee. Wherefore I abhor myself, and repent in dust and ashes" (Job 42:2–6). The Lord immediately turned to Job's friends and accused them of not speaking correctly as Job had done. After this the Lord not only restored Job's blessings, He gave Job double what he had before.

This episode is instructive. Obviously the Lord loved Job and felt he was a righteous individual. Yet when He saw the need, He severely chastised Job. Job's reaction was exactly what the Lord must have wanted. Job immediately humbled himself, and then He repented, wanting to change. This led to the Lord being able to bless Job more than he had been blessed before. What a valuable model from which we can learn. While I profess I don't fully understand this entire episode, I do see that God worked with Job in a way that could seem harsh but that produced the effect of helping Job progress, thus bringing about greater blessings for him.

Trusting God's Loving Plan for Us, or the Parable of the Sick Son

Sometimes as God works with us we won't understand what He is doing or why He is doing it. It is tempting to evaluate the way God works with us through our own limited mortal vision. Just as Job seems to have forgotten the majesty, awe, and wonder of the being we call God, so too it is easy for all of us to forget the degree to which God knows and understands us and how much He loves us. Forgetting these things can make our learning experiences slower and even more painful. We must remember that God wants only the best for us and knows better than we do how to work with us and help us get to where He wants us to be.

I came to understand this better when I was a young father. Our oldest child was just more than a year old when I started graduate school. We lived in Los Angeles in a little apartment a few miles away from UCLA. During our first year there, our little one-and-a half-year-old son became extremely ill. He went through several bouts of intense flu-like symptoms, getting better for a week or so only to relapse. During one of these bouts he had vomited so much for so long we knew he was in danger of serious dehydration. We eventually had to take him to an urgent care facility, where they put him on an intravenous saline solution in order to rehydrate him.

Before we took him to urgent care, I lay with him for hours on a little hide-a-bed we had in the front room. He had only learned to speak a few words at that age, but he could speak enough to let me know how dehydrated he was. For hours he just lay there saying, "Water, Daddy, water."

Sadly, he had gotten to the point where the least bit of liquid sent him into violent spasms of vomiting. I knew I could not give him any water because he would start a process that would leave him more dehydrated than before. It tore my heart out to hold him while he kept pleading and begging, "Water, Daddy, water."

During those long, painful hours I reflected on how our Heavenly Father must feel as we plead with Him. My son was right—he needed water. He could tell water would be a good thing for him and that if he didn't get it he would be in trouble. But he just didn't understand as much as I did. While he knew he needed water, he didn't realize as I did that the timing wasn't right. His lack of understanding made it so that he looked up at me wondering why I wouldn't help him when he knew I had the power to. It took all my inner strength not to give in to those pleading looks and his desperate importuning.

Later, when he was in the doctor's office full of fear, he looked at me trustingly as I held him still so that a nurse could insert a needle into his arm to deliver the desperately needed fluid. His shocked look of betrayal was difficult to take. He just didn't understand why I, who should have protected him, would actually help someone do something that hurt him. I don't know if he ever put that painful moment together with the relief he soon experienced as he received fluid.

I wonder how often I am like this with our Heavenly Father. I wonder how often I question something He does that makes no sense to me only because I fail to remember that I don't understand as much as He does. I think many times I must be asking for something that I know I need, but He knows that for some reason it is not the right time for it. I am convinced that often His heart breaks for us as He feels our desperation, yet He waits for the right time or He steers us patiently towards a path that is better. At other times He patiently insists that we be pierced by a painful needle that will deliver much-needed experiences.

The difference between the Lord's knowledge and understanding of things and my own is far greater than the difference between that of my one-year-old son and mine. Thus it should not be surprising that sometimes we neither understand nor like the ways the Lord works with us. However difficult it is for us and for Him, God will help us in the way that is best for us. We may look up at Him and plead, "Water, Father, water," knowing that we need what we ask for—but He will do that which is best for us. We may instead be asking Him to take some terrible thing away from us, but even if it hurts us and we don't understand it, He will do that which will lead us back to Him and to eternal life. We just have to have faith. We must believe that He loves us and that He knows what we need. Sometimes we won't like what He does or how He does it, but the truth is that His great love for us leads Him to do whatever is necessary to guide us back to Him—in His way. When God does lead us back—whether in the form of promptings, chastisement, pain, or opportunities—we must be "willing to submit to all things which the Lord seeth fit to inflict upon [us], even as a child doth submit to his father" (Mosiah 3:19).

Part of our ability to submit to the Father comes from knowing that He loves us and is only trying to help us. Another part stems from understanding how much more He sees and knows than we do. Joseph of Egypt provides a great example of this. Surely He could not see how the series of betrayals thrust upon him would help him to become great and enable him to rescue his family and innumerable others. Undoubtedly he could not see God's plan for him as it unfolded in such a strange way. But in hindsight he recognized it, telling his brothers, "be not grieved, nor angry with yourselves, that ye sold me hither: for God did send me before you to preserve life" (Gen. 45:5). Though Joseph may not have understood in the moment exactly why his Father denied him water or helped put an I.V. into his arm, he realized later that God knew exactly what He was doing.

Even the great prophet Elijah could not see all of God's workings. He once expressed to the Lord that he was the only one in all of Israel who served the Lord. The Lord responded to him that there were still seven thousand in Israel who served Him (see 1 Kgs. 19:18). Despite his great prophetic abilities, Elijah had not known that there were others on his side. Though he felt completely alone, he did not let his feeling or his incorrect knowledge prevent him from serving the Lord valiantly. He even competed with the king's priests in the midst of this feeling. We would do well to learn from Elijah. Though we may not know what the Lord knows, nor see what He sees, if we serve Him, perhaps even in ways that don't make sense to us, we will eventually find that He supports us in our efforts and that He knew what He was doing all along.

This is well illustrated by Elijah's prophetic successor, Elisha. Elisha, under the Lord's directions, used his prophetic abilities to help Israel avoid the enemy armies of Syria. The Syrians eventually decided that if they were to succeed against Israel, they first had to get rid of the prophet. So they sent their armies after Elisha and his servant. One morning these two men woke to find themselves surrounded by the entire Syrian army. This alarmed Elisha's servant, as I'm sure it would any of us. It would have been easy for them to ask how the Lord could allow them to be put in such circumstances when all they had ever done was try to follow His will. They could have easily complained that they had been abandoned and that this was a trial they should not have to go through. Instead, Elisha understood that there are realities present all around us of which we are often unaware. In a classic line, he told his servant, "they that be with us are more than they that be with them" (2 Kgs. 6:16). He then prayed that the Lord would open the servant's eyes, and the servant saw "the mountain was full of horses and chariots of fire round about Elisha" (2 Kgs. 6:17).

We too can be sure that the Lord is with us, even when we can't see or understand it. We can rest assured that the Lord's ways are higher than our ways and His thoughts are higher than our thoughts (see Isa. 55:8–9). This allows us to better submit to those things the

Lord does to us as He tries to help us return to Him. Though we may feel abandoned, even if we feel the way is too difficult and painful, we can know that the Lord is omnisciently and lovingly pushing us back to Him, surrounding us with unseen chariots of fire all the while.

Remembering that God knows and sees more than we do, and that His actions are guided by His love for us, can help us make sense of a number of seemingly harsh Old Testament stories. For example, the destruction of all mankind except for the family of Noah can seem a severe punishment. This vengeance is somewhat mollified when we remember that Noah warned them to repent or they would be destroyed for 120 years (see Moses 8:17) and that Enoch and others had been giving this warning for hundreds of years before that (see Moses 6:27–30). But it makes even more sense when we view the destruction through the knowledge that God loves His children and wants to help them return to Him. This understanding is conveyed in President John Taylor's suggestion that God brought about such destruction both to enable those spirits who were coming into the world to have the chance to be born into families that would teach them righteousness and to spare the wicked from the chance to commit further horrific acts against those spirits being born to them.[7] By ending their lives, God prevented them from bringing further justice upon themselves. Neither was the story over then, for these same spirits were given a chance to accept the gospel and repent in the spirit world (see D&C 138). By giving the world a clean slate, the Lord mercifully spared millions of spirits from coming into the world in the most horrible of situations—situations that would inevitably lead to misery. Seen from a larger perspective, it was a merciful flood.

We can also better understand the Lord's instructions to the children of Israel as they inherited the promised land. They were to destroy every Canaanite man, woman, and child—a complete and total destruction. Again, this seems harsh. Again, it is partially mollified when we learn that they had been repeatedly warned of impending destruction, yet had rejected that warning and had become ripe in iniquity (see 1 Ne. 17:33–35). But our understanding is enhanced even more when we see it as part of the same pattern illustrated in the flood. Not only was God preventing the Canaanites from committing further damning atrocities, but He was also creating an opportunity for Israel to grow up in righteousness. He warned Israel that if they did not fully destroy the Canaanites they would eventually partake of their idolatrous practices, such as child sacrifice and immorality, and that it would lead to their destruction (see Ex. 34; Deut. 7; Deut. 20). Thus, the destruction of the Canaanites was motivated by mercy for both the Canaanites and Israelites. Sadly the Israelites did not obey the Lord, and His warnings tragically came to pass. Israel was destroyed because they partook of the wicked traditions of those Canaanites they did not destroy. In this case the shortsighted mercy of Israel thwarted the farsighted mercy (though seeming harshness) of God.

This same perspective explains a number of Old Testament stories. Understanding the symbol-oriented nature of near eastern culture also helps. Once we understand that the Israelites were very symbol-oriented, and that symbolic action carried out by people was the most powerful form of communication, many elements of the Old Testament open to us. We are able to make sense of stories like the destruction of Lot's wife when we know that actions were interpreted as intentional messages and when we couple that with the knowledge that God wants to do what is best for us—even when it's hard for us. When Lot's wife turned to look at Sodom, it wasn't just a glance over the shoulder—it was a statement about where her heart and desires were. Had God not done anything about her gesture, it would have been a tacit acceptance, thus sending the wrong message to generations of offspring. While it was surely something that caused God to weep, He lovingly administered a painful lesson and turned her to salt (see Gen. 19).

Similarly, Miriam and Aaron involved themselves in an action that sent a powerful message to all of Israel. Knowing that they were also capable of communing with God and failing to understand how prophetic lines of authority worked, they complained about Moses being the one who received revelations from God for the whole host of Israel. In doing this, they tacitly proclaimed an incorrect doctrinal statement about how the Lord worked with prophetic leaders, even if that's not what they intended. If a symbolic action did not answer their misplaced actions, all of Israel would have learned the wrong lesson. A loving but firm father administered difficult justice by striking

Miriam with leprosy. In this case He was able to further extend mercy by healing her a short time later. His lesson had been taught in a way that did not need to be permanent (see Num. 12). Fortunately for Miriam, the Lord was able to teach a difficult but loving lesson and then mercifully spare her from the full force of that tutelage.

Sadly, this same lesson had to be taught again as a group of Israelites led by Korah contested Moses' prophetic authority. They challenged Moses in front of the entire congregation. This action spoke volumes to Israel, and the Lord had to answer in an equally loud way. He mercifully offered an opportunity for those who wanted to separate themselves from Korah to do so. Those who refused were swallowed up by a fissure in the earth. While this may seem harsh, the consequences of not sending a dramatic answer would have been cruelly harmful.

This is abundantly clear: Even with this vivid event, many in Israel murmured against Moses again the next day. Clearly the Lord had to do more to teach His children. He taught the lesson powerfully, sending a plague of death to Israel. He simultaneously allowed Aaron to make an atoning offering on behalf of Israel, halting the plague. In this situation the Lord lovingly taught Israel many lessons. He had again answered a symbolic action that challenged His prophet with a symbolic action that demonstrated the true principles of prophetic authority. He also taught powerfully of the Atonement of His Son, who would overcome death for us, by allowing Aaron to make an atoning sacrifice that halted death for Israel. It would have been distinctly unmerciful to allow Israel to learn the wrong message from Korah, which would surely have led to their destruction.

An echo to this story appears generations later in one of the oddest stories of the Bible. As Elijah ascended into heaven, His signature piece of clothing—a hairy mantle—fell upon Elisha. The two men had previously agreed that this would be the sign that Elisha was Elijah's prophetic successor. Elisha then used that mantle to part the Jordan River, just as Elijah had done before him. Clearly all of this was symbolic action designed to show that Elisha was now the Lord's prophet, in the same mold as Elijah. That hairy mantle served as the most tangible sign of prophetic succession; it colors our language even today when we speak of "the mantle falling" on someone who has been called by the Lord.

However, just after Elisha received the mantle, a group of rowdy teenagers challenged him. When they called him "bald," they were probably calling into question his ability to carry the hairy mantle. Most likely they were challenging his succession and rudely questioning his ability to follow Elijah. In essence, they were certainly mocking the newly called prophet. Had this action gone unanswered it would have spoken powerfully to all of Israel, indicating that God did not support Elisha as His prophet. Instead, the youth were consumed by bears. This seems harsh—but I am convinced that, like those in Noah's day, these youth will have their chance to repent. I also believe that in supporting His prophet in the symbolic language Israel looked for, God was mercifully helping Israel to follow the person God had sent to help them return unto Him.

These lessons are difficult. They are painful. They do not completely make sense to those of us who are so far removed in time and culture from those who were part of them. Coming to understand Israelite culture helps make some sense of them. Understanding that God helps bring His children home to Him through methods that will be most effective for them, regardless of how painful those methods may be, helps make more sense of them. Bears, leprosy, plagues, and fissures in the earth are like intravenous needles inserted into the arm of a child: painful, but spiritually life-saving. Clearly God saw these situations from a perspective far above ours and acted accordingly. Truly His thoughts are higher than ours and His ways higher than ours.

He Knew We Would Mess Up Again

As the Lord's covenant people were approaching the great destruction that justice brought them at the hands of Babylon, the Lord spoke through the prophet Jeremiah of His profound feelings for Israel and their great struggles: "Go and cry in the ears of Jerusalem, saying, Thus saith the Lord; I remember thee, the kindness of thy youth, the love of thine espousals, when thou wentest after me in the wilderness, in a land that was not sown. Israel was holiness unto the Lord, and the firstfruits of his increase. . . . And I brought you into a plentiful country, to eat the fruit thereof and the goodness thereof; but when ye entered, ye defiled my land, and made mine heritage an abomination" (Jer. 2:2–3, 7). Here we see the depth of the Lord's love again compared to the powerful affection and espousals between a newlywed couple. This helps us to understand the severity of His sadness when we stray and when we "defile" the blessings He has given us, turning them into "abominations."

Jeremiah helps us sense some of the Lord's dismay at our continual straying despite all He has done for us. After comparing their earlier relationship to the "love of thine espousals," the Lord asks, "What iniquity have your fathers found in me, that they are gone far from me, and have walked after vanity, and are become vain?" (Jer. 2:5). No one has found the Lord to be lacking in anything as a covenant partner, yet we still do things that take us further away from Him. Despite His incomparable love for us, we are repeatedly unfaithful in our covenant relationship with Him, often putting ourselves or something else ahead of the Lord.

Malachi also outlined how Israel did this: "Judah hath dealt treacherously, and an abomination is committed in Israel and in Jerusalem; for Judah hath profaned the holiness of the Lord which he loved, and hath married the daughter of a strange god" (Mal. 2:11). The important thing to remember is that the Lord's complaints given through Malachi came after Israel had sinned grievously, been punished severely, and returned to the Lord. Yet not long after the Lord accepted Israel back and rebuilt them as a nation, they again betrayed the covenant, "marrying the daughter of a strange god." We know that Israel did fall again and that they were punished again. We also know that they will eventually return, and the Lord will accept them yet again.

A vivid image of the Lord's punishments being directed at bringing us back is played out by Isaiah's family. When the Lord sent Isaiah to tell King Ahaz about the coming destruction of Syria and the northern kingdom of Israel, He told Isaiah to bring his son with him. These two met the king in the lower part of Jerusalem by the highway of the fuller's field. There Ahaz was assured that he need not worry about rumors of Syria and Israel overcoming him, for the Lord was about to destroy those two kingdoms (see Isa. 7:1–9). To underscore how quickly this would come, Isaiah prophesied that before a baby could grow old enough to become aware, the kingdoms would be destroyed. This prophecy was heightened by the fact that immediately thereafter Isaiah and his wife were blessed with another son, whom they named "Maher-shalal-hash-baz" (Isa. 8:3). This name, literally translated, means, "speed to the spoil, haste to the plunder." In other words, Israel would be destroyed very soon.

However, the prophecy about the destruction cannot be fully understood unless we remember the other son who was with Isaiah as he first spoke to the king about the imminent destruction. After all, the Lord had said that Isaiah and his children would be "for signs and wonders in Israel from the Lord of hosts" (Isa. 8:18). As Isaiah gave his prophecy, he had with him—through the Lord's commandment—his son Shear-Jashub. *Shear-Jashub* means "a remnant will **return**." To me this is so powerful. Though the Lord would have to punish Israel and even destroy them, He simultaneously made it clear that some of Israel would return. He very visually and vividly made both statements at the same time. It seems to me that He wants us all to know, even before His corrective measures come, that He wants to bring us back. When we feel the chastisement, we should remember the image of Isaiah standing there with His son, letting us know, even beforehand, that God wants us to return.

Just as Hosea accepted Gomer back after her repeated betrayals, and just as the Lord accepts Israel back after their repeated straying, He will accept us back even after we continue to mess up. He knew before we came here that we would vacillate in our faithfulness—that coming unto Him was a process with ups and downs, not a one-time event. He expects that it will take us time to become the kind of beings that are completely consistent and fully faithful. While we need to continually strive to do better, we can simultaneously be assured that the Lord will *always* be waiting for us, urging us to return to Him. We should be wholly confident that no matter how often we struggle with doing and being all we know we should do and be, the Lord is working with us, aiding our return, and ready to receive us and wrap us in the robes of righteousness and the outstretched arms of His love. This is part of His plan.

As President Thomas S. Monson has assured us, even during those times when we feel most alone or abandoned, we can turn to Heavenly Father in faith, knowing that He will life and guide us through whatever we face even if at times He will not remove our afflictions.[8] Would we expect anything less from a Father who loves us perfectly?

CHAPTER FOUR
IT IS NEVER TOO LATE

The LORD, the LORD God, merciful and gracious, longsuffering,
and abundant in goodness and truth,
Keeping mercy for thousands, forgiving iniquity
and transgression and sin.
(Ex. 34:6–7)

AT TIMES WE ALL ASK if our latest mistake demonstrates that we will just never make it. We all do one thing or another that causes us to ask if we really can become what God wants us to become. In this regard, President Dieter F. Uchtdorf taught an important lesson through an aviation analogy. He spoke of what pilots call the "point of safe return" or the "point of no return." This point is reached when a plane on a long journey, particularly over an ocean, has flown far enough that it no longer has enough fuel to return to its point of origin. When this point is reached there is no going back, no opportunity to return. President Uchtdorf then pointed out that Satan, the "father of all lies" (2 Ne. 2:18), wants us to believe that concept whenever we sin. He wants us to believe that it's too late to change course and that we cannot be forgiven (see Rev. 12:10). In his destructive and deceitful way, he even twists the words of scripture to convince us that God will mete out justice, but not mercy.[9]

President Uchtdorf continued his analogy in emphasizing our opportunity to return. Though a pilot who has passed the point of no return and then encountered difficulty must land somewhere other than his planned destination, our journey through life is different. In life, he pointed out, there is always a point of safe return because God has prepared a plan that will bring all of us safely back home—a plan that includes the Atonement of the Savior, which brings with it the possibility of repentance and forgiveness.[10]

Many of us create for ourselves a sense of hopelessness, or at least a feeling of unending frustration at our continual lack of measuring up to what we know we should do and be. We are aware of how much the Lord has blessed us. We have had powerful moments where He has shown us how we need to do better. We may have felt the Spirit so strongly that we have honestly not wanted to sin anymore—when, at least for a brief minute, "we have no more disposition to do evil" (Mosiah 5:2). Yet even after all these blessings and experiences, we do the same dumb things; we fall short in the same silly ways. Then we feel like we are a lost cause—after all, what more could the Lord do for us, and still we mess up. Given a pattern of falling short, why should either He or we expect that we would actually improve?

These feelings are particularly poignant when we keep repeating the same sin or keep failing to live up to our higher expectations. We are hit hardest when we have recognized a problem, repented, promised the Lord we wouldn't do it anymore, and then do it again, just to start the same cycle over. These repeated sins or failings can be of any kind. They can range from pornography to yelling unkindly at children; from failing to do home/visiting teaching to failing to be the kind of loving parent and spouse we would like to be. They can be as serious as immorality or as small as resentful envy. All of us find ourselves with some aspect of the gospel in which we frequently fail. Repeated failings often lead us to feel it is too late.

Worst of all is that we sometimes believe Satan's lies when he tells us that God doesn't love us. Our painful knowledge of ourselves, our feelings about our failings, and our natural shame at falling short make us fertile ground for Satan's damaging deception. He would have us believe that God loves others but not us. It is an outright lie but sometimes we fall for it. We prevent ourselves from feeling God's love. Because the entire plan of salvation is based on God's love for us, every other aspect of the plan falls apart when we cease to feel His love.

Separating ourselves from God's love is devastating. It is also totally unnecessary. There is absolutely nothing you can do or be that would stop God from loving you. You are fully incapable of becoming a being He does not love. Satan would have you believe that your repeated shortcomings make you unworthy of God's love. God would have you know that His love will never depart. God would have you return to His love no matter what you have done, for His love has always been there.

It Is Never Too Late

As already noted, the Lord knew we would be repeat offenders. This was built into the plan. Elder Jeffrey R. Holland spoke of this when He emphasized that no matter the problem, we can be helped, we can change, and we can be made whole because Christ has "borne our griefs, and carried our sorrows," and if we are willing, "with His stripes we are healed" through a God who has a forgiving disposition (see Isa. 53:4–5; Mosiah 14:4–5).[11]

We can more fully understand the concept that it is never too late if we learn lessons from the Old Testament and compare ourselves to ancient Israel. Let's delve more deeply into their story—seeing it as our own—and look for what the Lord said to His ancient people, understanding that He is also speaking to us. As the prophet who witnessed the destruction of Jerusalem, Jeremiah is particularly instructive as He speaks of the Lord's continual willingness to bring us back.

Look at Israel's position in Jeremiah's day. God had delivered His covenant people from Egypt through mighty miracles. Despite their problems in the wilderness, He had humbled them there until they were willing to be brought into the promised land. There He had blessed them and established them as a mighty people. Throughout this process, Israel had repeatedly turned away from God, yet He continually tried to bring them back to Him by sending prophetic warnings and by occasionally bringing them into captivity. He had unfailingly accepted their return and had preserved them, even in the face of seemingly undefeatable enemies such as the Assyrians. Despite all these things, Israel had become so wicked that they were on the brink of destruction—many of them had become seriously depraved.

Jeremiah outlines some of that depravity. Speaking for the Lord, he says of Israel, "My covenant they brake, although I was an husband unto them" (Jer. 31:32). Their sins had become so serious that the Lord described them like this: "The sin of Judah is written with a pen of iron, and with the point of a diamond: it is graven upon the table of their heart, and upon the horns of your altars" (Jer. 17:1). This is powerful imagery. Writing with iron and diamonds creates the strong impression that these sins are powerful, almost indelible. They have been written upon the very hearts of God's people, even into the symbols of Israel's covenant with God, such as the horns on the altar. Surely this passage is an attempt to illustrate to Israel, and to us, how serious their sins were.

Because of these serious sins—and presumably because they had been committed so often, despite all of God's kindness and mercy— Israel experienced a feeling of futility, saying "there is no hope: no; for I have loved strangers, and after them will I go" (Jer. 2:25). Here we sense something in ancient Israel many of us have felt ourselves. They seem to believe that they cannot give up their sins—that no matter how hard they try, they will continue to mess up in the same way. A sense of failure and a decision to give up seem to have pervaded the covenant people, as it so often does for each of us—perhaps in brief bouts or perhaps for lengthy periods of time.

Backsliding

One of the images Jeremiah frequently uses to describe Israel is that of a backsliding people. For example, the Lord asked Jeremiah, "Hast thou seen that which backsliding Israel hath done? she is gone up upon every high mountain and under every green tree, and there hath played the harlot" (Jer. 3:6). The Lord pleads with Israel to cease this habit, reminding them of their intimate relationship with him: "**Turn**, O backsliding children, saith the Lord; for I am married unto you" (Jer. 3:14). The idea of backsliding is employed by Jeremiah and Hosea more than fifteen times during Israel and Judah's last days before destruction. It is a very descriptive term—so aptly fitting the way Israel would make steps toward progress and then slip back into their wicked ways. What is disheartening for so many is that the term *backslider* fits most of us.

Who hasn't taken steps to become better, been successful for a while, and then slipped back into the same bad habits? Who hasn't repented, perhaps even repeatedly, and felt she had put some wicked practice or characteristic behind her, only to find that after a period of doing well she has slid back to the thing she swore she would never do again? We backslide, do better, and then backslide again. The term *backsliding* is so accurate in its ability to describe what we all do because it highlights our inconsistent ways.

One trend that can really take the wind out of our sails occurs when we are willing to take a candid, honest look at our backsliding. We are wont to use language such as, "I slipped into doing that again," or "I fell into that bad habit again." Confessions are full of phrases like "it happened," or "accidentally," or "I found myself doing. . . ." We like to use these words because we like to think in a certain way. We like to conceive of ourselves as passive in the bad things we do, in the ways we make mistakes, in the sins and shortcomings we repeat after having given them up. But deep inside we know these things don't just happen; they are the result of a choice. When we are frank enough with ourselves to realize this, it can be depressing—even hopeless.

We don't just happen to spend time looking at pornography. We don't just find ourselves falling into a gambling debt. We don't surrender control of our throats to some unseen power when we yell at our children. Lies, unkind words, rumors, and snide remarks don't just fall out of our mouth of their own accord. It is possible to fall asleep when we are supposed to be home teaching or at a meeting, but usually we are just too tired to make a call or too busy doing something else to think about it. The ways we backslide are results of choices we make. They happen of our own volition, whether we want to admit it or not. It is that element of backsliding that can be the most deflating. When we realize that our backsliding was something we *chose* to do, it can make us wonder if we possess the ability to keep making good choices. It can cause us to question whether God really wants us back when we have given in to our lower nature and chosen to rebel—to backslide.

Elder D. Chad Richardson addressed the feelings that can come from our continual backsliding. He pointed out that those caught in the cycle of sin tend to become discouraged—and that Satan uses that discouragement against us, even to a point of where we find solace in sin. At the complete opposite end of the spectrum is the Savior, who invites us to become free from sin when we fully repent and forgive ourselves.[12]

Again the Old Testament speaks to our current personal circumstances and provides answers. Jeremiah saw Israel during one of her greatest periods of wickedness, called Israel repeatedly to repentance, and used the term *backsliding* more than any other. As we already read, he accused Israel of backsliding and reminded them of their familial relationship with the Lord. He highlighted this many times, such as when the Lord said through Jeremiah, "Surely as a wife treacherously departeth from her husband, so have ye dealt treacherously with me, O house of Israel, saith the LORD" (Jer. 3:20). Like so many of us, Israel was aware of their wicked choices, as is seen in their collective confession: "We lie down in our shame, and our confusion covereth us: for we have sinned against the Lord our God, we and our fathers, from our youth even unto this day, and have not obeyed the voice of the Lord our God" (Jer. 3:25). Israel knew they were sinning, yet they continued to do so anyway. At one time or another we can all relate to this.

Many times we make a firm resolution to do better during the moments we feel the Spirit. Yet all too often when we are not feeling the Spirit and a moment of weakness comes, we choose to backslide. Sometimes we make poor choices even when we know we will regret them later, but at the moment we force those thoughts from our mind. We rationalize why in this instance, at this time, in this circumstance, it is different and okay—even though deep down we know we are lying to ourselves. Or sometimes we just choose not to care—and then we backslide.

When we lose our good resolve and willfully rebel like this, we can be compared to Israel when the Lord said, "Thus saith the Lord, Stand ye in the ways, and see, and ask for the old paths, where is the good way, and walk therein, and ye shall find rest for your souls. But they said, We will not walk therein. Also I set watchmen over you, saying, Hearken to the sound of the trumpet. But they said, We will not hearken" (Jer. 6:16–17). Those weak moments, when we know that it is better to go another way but choose not to, are like refusing to find rest for our souls! Israel's refusal to listen to the trump of the watchman parallels those times we ignore feelings deep within that indicate something we are about to do is not a good idea! All too often we find ourselves backsliding like Israel in Jeremiah's day.

Healing Our Backsliding

Even in the midst of their continual backsliding, rampant treachery, and lack of faithfulness, the Lord hastened to assure Israel that He would have them back if they would just come to Him. To this wicked group, the Lord said, "**Return**, ye backsliding children, and I will heal your backslidings" (Jer. 3:22; emphasis added). In saying this, the Lord extends such promise! Despite Israel's willful sins, the Lord still pleads with them to **return** to him. But more than this, He promises to heal their backslidings.

I see God healing that backsliding as at least a three-fold healing process: first, I believe it means that the Lord will forgive them of their sins; second, I think He is offering to heal them from the spiritual wounds they have experienced as a result of those sins; and third, I think it implies that the power of the Atonement can heal the children of Israel from being the kind of people that backslide. I am convinced that part of the healing process our great Savior offers us is the ability to change our nature—to help us become someone who backslides less and less, until we stop backsliding. That is real healing. As we read in one of our hymns—"O Savior, Thou Who Wearest a Crown"—none of us is so lowly or depraved that we can't be saved through Christ's and love and regain His presence.[13]

A Patience that Does Not End

The Lord knows that bringing us back to Him after we have strayed will not be a one-time experience. He has gone through this many times with Israel as they repeated a cycle of turning to the Lord, being blessed, turning away, and then experiencing punishments that brought them back to God. This is the recurrent story of Israel in the Bible, of Israel in the Book of Mormon, and of a chosen group in the book of Ether. Thus we can see that God is not a stranger to our struggles to consistently come unto Him. He has seen it before, many times, and knows we will go through this struggle. Our rebellion surely saddens Him, but His great parental love ensures that He is unendingly there to help us come back. He is not looking for a chance to say that it is too late, that we have done poorly too many times. He is a loving parent who desperately wants to bring us home, however hard the trek. As Joseph Smith taught, "the Great Parent of the universe looks upon the whole of the human family with a fatherly care and a paternal regard; He views them as His offspring."[14] This Heavenly Parent, whose love for us exceeds our ability to comprehend, knew that even after He had worked with us we would still sometimes—maybe frequently—fall short, turn away, repeat sins, or seek after the wrong things.

Think about that image of a loving God who is trying to help. Have you ever disciplined a young child who did something wrong? After being punished, has she ever looked up at you, waiting for you to hug her because she wanted to feel that you still loved her? If so, then of course you hugged her, because of course you still loved her. And we are but imperfect parents with an imperfect love.

Think of our "Great Parent" who feels a fatherly care and paternal regard for us in a perfect way, with a greater capacity for love than we can comprehend. Of course He still loves us, no matter how often we mess up. Of course He is waiting to hug us. He *will* discipline us, because He wants to bring us back to Him. When I discipline my three-year-old, I often find myself loving her all the more, wanting so badly for her to do it right as I take her in my arms, hold her, and help her feel how much I love her. I imagine this is how God feels—to a much greater degree—when He disciplines us.

Let's retrace our steps just a little. We must remember that the healing we have spoken of begins with justice. We must also remember that justice is aimed at bringing us back. Prophetic Jeremiah said to backsliding Israel, "I beheld, and, lo, the fruitful place *was* a wilderness, and all the cities thereof were broken down at the presence of the Lord, and by his fierce anger. For thus hath the LORD said, The whole land shall be desolate; *yet will I not make a full end*" (Jer. 4:26–27; emphasis added). While the coming destruction must have been a frightening vision, the promise is that it was not the end for Israel—the Lord was holding out more chances for repentance. Because this point was so important, the Lord had Jeremiah make it again and again.

Note how the Lord tells Israel, through Jeremiah, the reason for the coming vengeance, yet He again reassures them that it will not be a full destruction. He also says, "How shall I pardon thee for this? thy children have forsaken me, and sworn by them that are no gods: when I had fed them to the full, they then committed adultery, and assembled themselves by troops in the harlots' houses. They were as fed horses in the morning: every one neighed after his neighbour's wife. Shall I not visit for these things? saith the Lord: and shall not my soul be avenged on such a nation as this? Go ye up upon her walls, and destroy; *but make not a full end*" (Jer. 5:7–10; emphasis added).

Aren't our lives sometimes like this? Can't we often identify how the Lord has fed us full—full of blessings and teachings beyond what we deserve? And yet, from time to time, we still choose to turn aside. The comforting thing is that when we reap the consequences for this, we can be sure it is not the end. The story isn't over. God is reaching out to us still.

Remember how the Lord told Hosea that He would take away the good things Gomer sought after so she would remember she could get them only from the Lord? Taking them away did not mean she could never have them back—these good things were not at an end. Gomer just needed to seek them from the Lord, and then they were hers for the asking. He said essentially the same thing to Israel through Jeremiah, speaking of the destruction other nations would bring to Israel: "And they shall eat up thine harvest, and thy bread, which thy sons and thy daughters should eat: they shall eat up thy flocks and thine herds: they shall eat up thy vines and thy fig trees: they shall impoverish thy fenced cities, wherein thou trustedst, with the sword. Nevertheless in those days, saith the Lord, *I will not make a full end with you*" (Jer. 5:17–18; emphasis added).

I suspect that for most of us our sins are not as great as ancient Israel's, and our punishments will not be as severe. Thus we can safely conclude that if the end of blessings and opportunities did not come to Israel, they will not come to us. Just as the Lord worked with Israel, He will work with us. This makes the Lord's pleadings and extension of mercy to Israel all the more meaningful and poignant for us. Look at what He tells our ancient counterparts: "Go and proclaim these words toward the north, and say, **Return**, thou backsliding Israel, saith the LORD; and I will not cause mine anger to fall upon you: for I am merciful, saith the LORD, and I will not keep anger forever" (Jer. 3:12).

This verse is powerful in several ways. First, it tells us that despite all of Israel's terrible and continuous backsliding, the Lord wanted them to return and promised mercy if they did. This is even more compelling when we remember that the Lord was accusing Israel of adultery, murder, and worshipping false gods. How amazing it is that He still offered them mercy. The reason why He would do so is also revealed in this verse.

A student of mine once pointed out what this verse tells us about the character of God, and thus the reasons for His actions.[15] In this verse He tells us that He *has* anger, and He *keeps* it, but it is not what He is. In strong contrast, He *is* merciful. Anger is something He *has*, while mercy embodies who He *is*. Because of His love and mercy He uses wrath and justice with Israel, all aimed at bringing them back to Him. This is true even when Israel repeatedly turned to the worst of sins after continual and abundant blessings and after incessant backsliding. How comforting to know that it was not too late for Israel, because it means it is not too late for you or me!

President Dieter F. Uchtdorf taught that those who believe they can no longer fully partake of the blessings of the gospel don't understand the purposes of the Lord. The blessings of the gospel help refine us by helping us learn from our mistakes, and the Atonement has the power to make us whole when we fully repent.[16]

Sometimes we feel the worst about backsliding when we realize that we know better. When we consider how much we have been blessed, how much the Lord has trusted us, and how much He has taught us, backsliding seems all the worse. It is true—because we have been given great knowledge, we should do better. But the Lord anticipated even this. He knew that those who were progressing toward Him would most often do so inconsistently. Consider what He said to the spiritual leaders of Israel: "The priests said not, Where *is* the LORD? and they that handle the law knew me not: the pastors also transgressed against me, and the prophets prophesied by Baal, and walked after things that do not profit" (Jer. 2:8). Think of this— those very people who were supposed to lead Israel *to* God were leading them *away*. What a terrible betrayal of trust.

But even in this circumstance the Lord wanted to help His people. He continued by saying, "Wherefore I will yet plead with you, saith the LORD, and with your children's children will I plead" (Jer. 2:8–9). Think of how merciful and patient the Lord is when we see Him pointing out the terrible sins of His leaders and simultaneously saying He will continue to plead with both them and their children. Even for those who were so spiritually adulterous it was not too late.

Fortunately we are able to more fully see this through the Joseph Smith Translation of Jeremiah. There, after all of Israel's great sins, the Lord said, "Thy bruise is not incurable, although thy wounds are grievous" (JST Jer. 30:12). What Israel had done gave them a grievous wound, just as we often bring unthinkable injury to our souls. But even then the wound was not incurable. As we have already seen, the Lord stood ready to heal their backsliding. It is reminiscent of the voice the Nephites heard after the Savior's death. After all the Lord had done for them time after time, they fell into grievous iniquity and reaped judgment and destruction as a result. Yet even then the Lord said, "Will ye not now **return** unto me, and repent of your sins, and be converted, that I may heal you?" (3 Ne. 9:13; emphasis added). If the Lord still extended mercy to these groups after so many blessings and so much wrongdoing, I believe He will extend it to you and me—regardless of how many times we fall short.

Sometimes the need to go back to the Lord and tell Him that we have yet again fallen short is a dreadful prospect. After falling off whatever wagon we have gotten on—again—coming before the Lord to talk about it may be the last thing we want to do. His perfection and justice, when compared with our stupidity and sins, can make us fear coming to Him. This was illustrated by Elder Jeffrey R. Holland as He recounted the time the apostles were on a boat and saw a figure walking on the water, which caused them fear. He likened that to our first step in coming to Christ, something that can make us afraid, even though it shouldn't. He pointed out the irony that we might actually flee from the thing that would actually give us the greatest succor and safety.[17] This will almost always be the case when we concentrate on what we have done and on God's justice.

However, what we have read from the Old Testament should help us avoid this feeling of fright. God's unending willingness to work with relentlessly rebellious Israel should convince us that it is never too late for us. The teachings of ancient Israel's prophets should fully persuade us that whatever we have done, and however many times we have done it, God stands ready to accept us back, to heal us, to take us in, and to build us up. While He would like for us to quit backsliding, He is not surprised when we do, and He is not about to give up on us. If He can be confident that Israel will come back to him, He can believe you will as well. If He stands ready to forgive a generation of murderers and adulterers after having delivered them and forgiven them countless times, He stands ready to forgive me when I repeatedly go back on my promise to do better. His atoning power and abundant mercy are greater than my ability to turn away and backslide. My inconsistency is no match for His constancy, and the force of my failures pales in comparison to the power of His love and Atonement.

That is why President Boyd K. Packer, when speaking of the light and power of the Atonement, said that no amount of wickedness can quench the light of the Savior and the promise of His ransom—and that all who have ever lived can choose to touch the light and make claim on that redemption.[18] That includes you and it includes me, no matter how many times we have backslid.

I am not subscribing to some kind of universalism. Some advocate that God's all-powerful love for us combined with His great ability to save us means that God will eventually save everyone, universally. While I have no doubt God would love to save us all, He also honors our agency. Some will chose not to let God save them. But I believe that God will save all who will *let* Him save them. Why would He ever stop trying? Why would a Father so full of love say that you and I could not start over and try again, if we are willing? I believe that as long as we are willing to try again He is willing to help us again. He will heal us of our backsliding, take us back as a prodigal, and extend His saving grace if we will just accept it. He is always willing and waiting, no matter how we have messed up.

Elder Joseph B. Wirthlin summed it up so well when He taught, "Oh, it is wonderful to know that our Heavenly Father loves us— even with all our flaws! His love is such that even should we give up on ourselves, He never will."[19]

The great comfort is that God is willing to receive His children if they come back to Him. Through Ezekiel, who was prophesying to captives in Babylon while Jeremiah was prophesying in Jerusalem, the Lord spoke to His wicked and abased people. The Lord told Israel that one day they would return—and that when that day came, He would gather them in and take care of them Himself. When they would cease to "defile themselves any more with their idols, nor with their detestable things, nor with any of their transgressions: but I will save them out of all their dwelling places, wherein they have sinned, and will cleanse them: so shall they be my people, and I will be their God. And David my servant *shall be* king over them; and they all shall have one shepherd: they shall also walk in my judgments, and observe my statutes, and do them" (Ezek. 37:23–24). When Israel would repent so God could cleanse them, He would then build them up, establish them: "Moreover I will make a covenant of peace with them; it shall be an everlasting covenant with them: and I will place them, and multiply them, and will set my sanctuary in the midst of them for evermore. My tabernacle also shall be with them: yea, I will be their God, and they shall be my people" (Ezek. 37:26–27).

What touching language! The Lord paints a picture of such intimate care and such a bonding relationship. In the midst of their greatest tragedy, a result of their wickedness, the Lord had His prophet promise Israel that when they chose to follow Him, He would yet be their caregiver—He was ready once again to take them under His wing and bless them with peace.

Think of that promise in our own lives. The Lord has made it clear that while we have all done things to estrange ourselves from Him, He is there, waiting and anxious to bless us with peace and to care for us. Of this we can be sure: We cannot believe that anything we have done has permanently separated us from God. If only we will repent and return, He will give us peace, multiply us, and be in our midst. What we are like right now is irrelevant. God loves us so much that He will take us as we are. It is what we can become that He is concerned with. As President Thomas S. Monson has told us so many times, our great worth is in our capacity to become as God is.[20]

Second Chances

God's desire to help us reach our full capacity is demonstrated by His continual willingness to extend wicked Israel yet one more chance to return to Him, as He did so often through Jeremiah and

Ezekiel. This theme is not only featured through the story of the Old Testament as a whole, but in dozens of small stories throughout that book. Consider, for example, the story of Joseph's brothers. Here was a group so full of envy of their brother that they were willing to either kill him or sell him into slavery to be rid of him. The Lord, probably through promptings of guilt and a variety of difficult circumstances, must have worked on them to get them to change and regret what they had done. This is illustrated when Joseph first met them and they found themselves in difficult circumstances. They said to each other, "we are verily guilty concerning our brother, in that we saw the anguish of His soul, when He besought us, and we would not hear; therefore is this distress come upon us" (Gen. 42:21).

Joseph's brothers were given a second chance, another opportunity to see if the strivings of the Spirit had made a big enough difference in them that they would react differently in the same circumstances. It is clear that Benjamin had replaced Joseph as their father's favorite. He was so clearly favored by their father that Jacob was willing to let Simeon rot in an Egyptian prison rather than risk losing Benjamin. Undoubtedly Benjamin's brothers saw in him the same things that had caused them to hate and sell Joseph.

At that point, Joseph gave them the perfect opportunity to get rid of Benjamin. This time they would not have to lie or do anything wrong. In fact, all they had to do was nothing. They would be able to return to Jacob and tell them they had done everything they could, but that Benjamin had been so foolish as to steal a silver cup from an Egyptian leader—something that was out of their control. If they had been the same men they were when they sold Joseph, they would have taken advantage of this golden opportunity and been rid of another favored brother.

But these men had changed. In fact, Judah—the architect of selling Joseph—is the one who most fully demonstrated that change. When given a second chance to see how he would do in a difficult situation, Judah passed with flying colors. He offered to take Benjamin's place (see Gen. 44:33). Instead of getting rid of his little brother, he would take upon himself Benjamin's punishment. Rather than make his father suffer again, he would give away his own life. It was a second chance well used.

In a later story we see the Lord extending a second chance to Israel as a whole. When the Lord helped Israel conquer Jericho, they were instructed to leave alone the gold and goods of the city. Achan disobeyed and took some of it for himself, hiding it in his tent (see Josh. 7:1). The very next time Israel went against the Canaanites, Israel was soundly defeated—a result of not fully obeying the Lord.

However, that was not the end of the story. The Lord didn't just give them that one try and abandon them when they blew it. He allowed them to do their best to make things right and try again.

When it was discovered that Achan had taken that which he shouldn't have, the Israelites did not take any chances with the Lord's mercy. Instead of taking half measures, they destroyed everything and everyone connected to that sin, completely putting it away. Once this was done, they tried again. In this second chance the Lord was with Israel, and they were victorious over the people of Ai. If there had been ten people who had taken the goods of Jericho into their tents, and if it had taken Israel ten times to find all the sinful objects within them, I suspect the Lord would have still worked with them and given them ten chances. So will He do with us in our repeated efforts to put our sins away from ourselves.

Elsewhere in the Old Testament we find a story full of second chances to return to the Lord. The opportunity to try again after messing up is perhaps best exemplified in the story of Jonah.[21] At the beginning of the episode it is clear that the Assyrian inhabitants of Nineveh have been wicked and have been warned of the judgment that will come from their wickedness. Because God so deeply desires His children to repent, He always warns them multiple times, making repeated efforts to bring them back before judgment comes. Harsh judgments usually don't come until the group has become ripe in iniquity and has ignored many warnings and pleadings from God. The story makes it seem as if Nineveh is being sent its last warning in the form of Job. Thus the story begins with a repeatedly wicked group being given another chance to come unto God. They still have time to repent and be forgiven for having so seriously messed up.

Ironically, the messenger chosen to give them this last chance ends up in need of a second chance himself. Jonah chooses to rebel against God and run away from his appointed task. Sometimes we fail to fulfill assignments from the Lord because we forget, because we are too lazy to quite get around to it, or because other things are perceived as higher priorities. Other times we don't do what we ought because we just choose not to; sometimes we even refuse and stay far away from what we have been asked to do. Jonah is an extreme example of the latter case. He seems to be consciously running as far away from Nineveh as he can. He outright refuses to do what God asks of him.

Inevitably, judgment comes to Jonah because of his unwillingness. It would seem to be a rather severe judgment. A storm arose at sea that brought dire consequences to Jonah and everyone who was associated with him, even those accidentally wrapped up in the events. However, as we have seen so many times, this was not justice without reason. It was justice meant to put Jonah in a situation that would pressure him toward repentance. It worked. In the belly of the great fish, Jonah realized that the Lord was calling him to repentance—giving him a second chance to fulfill his mission. To his credit, Jonah took advantage of that second chance. He changed and went to Nineveh to extend to them their second chance.

Like their messenger, this great and wicked city took advantage of God's mercy. After all they had done, the Ninevites started over, trying to come unto God. They messed up, repeatedly, but at last they took advantage of God's longsuffering and loving kindness and turned back to Him.

Poor Jonah did not like this turn of events—imagine you have been called on a mission to Al-Quaeda and that you succeeded in helping them escape judgment. Jonah could not quite get himself to feel the charity that would lead him to be pleased with the repentance of the Ninevites. But the Lord did not give up on His recalcitrant prophet. He continued working with Jonah, giving him shade and then taking it away again in an attempt to teach Jonah about his misplaced mercies. When He does so, the Lord reveals His feelings about the continually sinning Ninevites: "Then said the Lord, Thou hast had pity on the gourd, for the which thou hast not laboured, neither madest it grow; which came up in a night, and perished in a night: And should not I spare Nineveh, that great city, wherein are more than sixscore thousand persons that cannot discern between their right hand and their left hand; and also much cattle?" (Jonah 4:10–11). The Lord wanted Jonah to see that these people, His children, meant more to Him than a gourd. They did not seem to be very educated in the ways of right and wrong, and the Lord wanted to teach them and give them the chance to do things right. In short, He loved them and wanted to help them.

We do not know how Jonah reacted to this message. What we can see is that from beginning to end, the book of Jonah is about God giving people another chance. No matter how much they knew of the things of God—the Ninevites knew little, and presumably Jonah knew much—no matter the rebelliousness behind their decisions, God worked with His people in a way designed to turn them about, to bring them back home. He put them in circumstances that would humble them. He taught them and worked to make them better than before. He gave them another chance. If He did so with Nineveh, if He he did so with Jonah, won't He do so with us?

CHAPTER FIVE
OUR CURRENT STATE DOESN'T MATTER

I trust in the mercy of God for ever and ever.
(Ps. 52:8)

Passing Over Who We Are for Who We Will Be

BACKSLIDING AND BLOWING SECOND CHANCES are not the only things that cause us to feel hopeless about our ability to come to God. We also face our painfully abundant knowledge about ourselves. Often we are not reassured by what others say about our celestial potential because they don't know us the way we know ourselves. They don't know the less-than-ideal feelings we often have. They don't know the temptations with which we struggle. They don't know our shortcomings like we do. They haven't seen us at our worst moments. Others aren't aware of the promises we have made to God and then broken time after time. They aren't familiar with all of the things we have done wrong, or with the characteristics we possess that are so un-Godlike. Others just don't know.

But God does. And He loves us anyway. In some ways He may love us more because we have these shortcomings and struggle to approach Him nonetheless. Feeling down or hopeless about who we really are stems from a lack of understanding two things. The first is God's love; the second is His power. As I have come to understand these things—most especially by studying the Old Testament and characters like Gomer, Jeremiah, and Ezekiel—the power of God's love has wiped out negative feelings. There is no room for such doubts; God's love fills everything and leaves no place for them.

We must not allow ourselves to believe, even for a minute, that whatever state we are in, even at our worst moments, it is a state too abject for God to love us or too low for God to help us. Such is never the case. It doesn't matter what you have done or where you are—God loves you and can make of your messy life a beautiful garden. This is illustrated well when we contrast the state of Jerusalem's inhabitants in the height of their wickedness and the promise Zechariah extended to them afterward.

Zechariah was a prophet sent to help the Jews who had returned from Babylonian captivity; though they had been eminently wicked, they were in the process of trying to return to the Lord. One of his major thrusts was to help them rebuild the temple.

Zechariah's message is one of hope and comfort. His name, which means "Jehovah remembers" or "remembered of Jehovah," sums up his message in many ways. After the difficulties of the Exile, God assured His people that He remembered them and wanted them to return to Him. He continually offered them the opportunity to put the sins of the past behind them, to start anew, and to receive all the blessings He wanted to give them.

Zechariah's visions symbolized how God gave His people another chance and teach us much about God's dealings with us. Historically, Israel had suffered great tribulation. They had lost their treasured city, their land, their freedom, and their ability to perform their holiest rites because their most precious possession, the temple, had been destroyed. Israel experienced these trials because they had repeatedly rejected the warnings of the prophets and had continually transgressed. After a generation had passed, the Lord opened the door for them to return to Jerusalem, and they set out to rebuild the temple.

It was at this time that Zechariah saw his visions. In the first vision, he saw horsemen who had gone throughout all the earth and found peace. Zechariah was told that this meant the Lord was bringing Israel back—that He would show them great mercies, would again comfort Zion, and would choose Jerusalem (see Zech. 1:16–17). As I read this I can picture the Lord speaking to me. After having made covenants with God, I have repeatedly gone astray. I have messed up and been distracted by the things of the world. Yet if I will turn to the Lord (see Zech. 1:3), He will yet show me great mercies. Though I have made the same mistake time and again, He will comfort me and I can yet be chosen of Him.

In order to appreciate the contrast between our current state and the state God offers us, we must compare ourselves to the state of Jerusalem after the Babylonian destruction and the rebuilding of the city Zechariah was speaking of. Jeremiah describes for us Jerusalem's fallen condition when he lamented, "How doth the city sit solitary, that was full of people! how is she become as a widow!" (Lam. 1:1). This state resulted from Zion's wickedness and the incumbent judgments of the Lord: "How hath the Lord covered the daughter of Zion with a cloud in his anger, and cast down from heaven unto the earth the beauty of Israel, and remembered not his footstool in the day of his anger!" (Lam. 2:1).

Jeremiah goes on to explain the cause and effect of Jerusalem's situation: "We have transgressed and have rebelled: thou hast not pardoned. Thou hast covered with anger, and persecuted us: thou hast slain, thou hast not pitied. Thou hast covered thyself with a cloud, that our prayer should not pass through. Thou hast made us as the offscouring and refuse in the midst of the people. All our enemies have opened their mouths against us. Fear and a snare is come upon us, desolation and destruction. Mine eye runneth down with rivers of water for the destruction of the daughter of my people. Mine eye trickleth down, and ceaseth not, without any intermission, Till the Lord look down, and behold from heaven" (Lam. 3:42–50).

Undoubtedly, this describes our lives sometimes. We transgress and rebel. We know better and still do wrong. The Lord asks us to do something, and we fail to do it. And then we feel that separation from the Lord—we are cut off and feel as if we have become refuse, as if we have stepped into desolation and destruction. Sometimes the chaos around us seems to spiral out of control until our eyes run with rivers. Yet along with Jeremiah, we can wait until the Lord will look down and behold us from heaven.

The timing of when the Lord will look down is somewhat up to us. In Zechariah we learn that after Jerusalem's destruction the Lord was waiting for Israel to turn to Him again. In chapter 8 He reinforces what will happen to Jerusalem when they do so: "Thus saith the Lord; I am **returned** unto Zion, and will dwell in the midst of Jerusalem: and Jerusalem shall be called a city of truth; and the mountain of the Lord of hosts the holy mountain. Thus saith the Lord of hosts; There shall yet old men and old women dwell in the streets of Jerusalem, and every man with his staff in his hand for very age. And the streets of the city shall be full of boys and girls playing in the streets thereof" (Zech. 8:3–5; emphasis added). Think of the joyful image that is associated with watching children play. Sometimes our lives feel devoid of this joy; they feel more like Jeremiah's description of solitude—like that experienced by a widow. However, Zechariah teaches us that if we turn to the Lord to the best of our ability, He will make us whole, just as He did Jerusalem. The emptiness will be filled with joy as wonderful as the sound of children playing and laughing.

Zechariah's message becomes even more personal in another of his visions. He saw the priest Joshua surrounded by an angel on one side and Satan on the other. Satan had obviously had some effect on Joshua, as illustrated by his appearance. His garments were full of muck and filth. Surely we have all felt this way sometimes. There are days, weeks, and months where we feel that devils and angels are enticing us. Sometimes we give in to those devils and become dirty. We have all had some kind of experience where it seemed as if in the presence of an angel we stood in stinking, rotting, filthy robes. In some ways this image is accurate. Our sins have made us filthy; we have figuratively played in the muck and wallowed in the mire. But the story does not have to end there.

In Zechariah's vision we learn of the chance for cleansing we all have. The Lord rebuked Satan for Joshua's sake. Then the Lord told the priest, who was still standing in filth in the presence of an angel, that they would "take away the filthy garments from him. And unto him he said, Behold, I have caused thine iniquity to pass from thee, and I will clothe thee with change of raiment. And I said, Let them set a fair mitre upon his head. So they set a fair mitre upon his head, and clothed him with garments. And the angel of the Lord stood by" (Zech. 3:4–5).

This vision gives such a sense of comfort. While we have all been in the muck, we have the chance to have that filth taken away. The power of the Atonement allows the Lord to "remove the iniquity of that land in one day" (Zech. 3:9).

When the Lord tells us of the cleansing of Jerusalem, or the purifying of Joshua, He is telling us He will do the same for you and me. Cleansing is available. The conditions given to Joshua were simple: "If thou wilt walk in my ways, and if thou wilt keep my charge" (Zech. 3:7). If you and I will try to walk in the Lord's ways, He will cleanse us and crown us. The depth of your filth is not an issue; the Lord can cleanse you from anything. The mitre awaits, the cleansing is just around the corner. It is available to all. The Lord promised ancient Israel and you that "they shall be my people, and I will be their God, in truth and in righteousness," and that we can have "joy and gladness and cheerful feasts" (Zech. 8:8, 19).

Personal Tutoring

Sometimes we feel like the kind of joy and gladness the Lord promises is available only for people who are far more perfect than we. We may think, *These things are the prizes for men like Job, or perhaps for Noah, but not for me. Such men were worthy of God's blessings because of what they had become.* What we forget is that we can all become like the great men of the scriptures, and even greater, if we will let the Lord take us there. A modern symbolic example may help us view these feelings in the right light.

In our day, many people turn to a personal trainer in their efforts to become different physically. The personal trainer is not hired because he can transform only one body type. Instead we hire someone because we believe he will assess where we are physically and determine what we need to do to become physically better than we are. The trainer creates a specific plan for each person that is designed to help her, step by step, go from wherever she is physically to a higher place. If we follow the plan we get the results. If we stop following the plan, even thirty times, it does not mean that we can never get in good physical shape. It may become harder to reach our fitness goal, but if we start back on the plan we can get there.

The Lord is much more capable of helping us become spiritually fit than a personal trainer is able to aid our physical progress. God knows you, and He knows what needs to happen for you to become something better. Furthermore, while there may be limitations to our physical success, there are no limitations to our spiritual success. While a trainer will never be able to make me taller, God can actually change my spiritual nature. Due to the genetic structure of my knees and damage I have sustained, no trainer will ever succeed in getting me to jump very high. Yet no such restrictions can bind the Lord in enhancing my spiritual growth. He can undo damage and change my makeup. The trainer cannot make my body soar like that of Michael Jordan, but the Lord can change my spiritual character so that I can soar beyond what I am capable of now. He knows my needs, my limitations, and my potential. He can give me personalized experiences to help me train spiritually, and He can change my nature when I am not personally able to make the kinds of changes that need to come. As Elder Neal A. Maxwell said, "Thus, the whole mortal schooling process has been so carefully structured to achieve results which could be achieved in 'no other way.' (Hel. 5:9.) We can come to know the Lord as our loving, tutoring Father and God."[22]

God's personal plan for you and me will never become obsolete. His plan will always work for you whenever you are willing to come back. By no means am I suggesting that we should be casual about how hard and how consistently we are trying to follow the Lord's plan for us. When we fail to follow God there is always an inherent danger that we won't return to the path of righteousness. Moreover, pauses in progress inevitably cause pain for others and for us. Nevertheless, when we do struggle, if we do pause, the spiritual fitness plan will still work if we take it up again. The Atonement can transform us, and God will always take us back into His program.

Because He knows we have weaknesses, foibles, and character flaws, and because He loves us so much, the Lord is perfectly willing to work with us in those weaknesses. We often imagine we must rid ourselves of some shortcoming before we can really work with the Lord, or that He requires us to serve Him without those weaknesses before He will magnify us in our work. This is simply not the case. He will work with us and help us in whatever state we are, as long as we will let Him.

As Elder Maxwell said, "God does not begin by asking us about our ability, but only about our availability, and if we then prove our dependability, He will increase our capability!"[23] To this I would add that your chances to prove your dependability do not disappear if you have blown it thus far. Your ability and what you have done in the past do not determine God's willingness to help you. His *love* determines that willingness. His *opportunity* to help is determined by *when* we demonstrate our availability and dependability. We will all experience degrees of intermittence in our dependability, but whenever we are willing to try again, God is ready.

There are times when we all wonder if we are worthy to approach God. We know that in reality we are not, and we do not possess the capability to approach Him. Yet we have been commanded to come unto Him. I think this is the reason the brother of Jared ceased to pray unto the Lord. The Lord chastised him for three hours because "he remembered not to call upon the name of the Lord" (Ether 2:14).

Why would such a great man fail to continue coming unto the Lord? I suspect we learn at least part of the answer when he does come unto the Lord in prayer on Mount Shelem. There, the first thing the brother of Jared says to the Lord is, "O Lord, thou hast said that we must be encompassed about by the floods. Now behold, O Lord, and do not be angry with thy servant because of his weakness before thee; for we know that thou art holy and dwellest in the heavens, and that we are unworthy before thee; because of the fall our natures have become evil continually; nevertheless, O Lord, thou hast given us a commandment that we must call upon thee, that from thee we may receive according to our desires" (Ether 3:2).

Here we can see the dilemma the brother of Jared feels deep within himself. He has a huge problem: He and his people must cross deep water, but floods will overcome them. In order to solve this problem, the brother of Jared needs help. Yet he fears to come before the Lord to ask for help because he has come to realize the great gulf between his own state of being and that of the Lord's. He knows that, however righteous he may strive to be, his nature is evil because of the Fall, and he is unworthy before the Lord. Thus he fears that a being who is so holy will be angry because of his own unholy, mortal weaknesses. I believe this conviction of his unworthiness and the fear of the difference between himself and God led the brother of Jared to fear calling on God. But now he has been chastened for that fear, so after expressing his need and his knowledge of his unworthiness to come before the Lord seeking help, the brother of Jared acknowledges that he has been commanded to seek his desires from the Lord.

Stated elsewise, recognizing his fallen nature and unworthy character, the brother of Jared would never have come to the Lord for help, except that the Lord told him that he must. Therefore, he dutifully came. Too many of us get stuck in the first part of this example—the knowledge of our own ungodliness—and never overcome it enough to follow God's command to come unto him. Of course we are not worthy; no one is. But God is not concerned with that; He can make us worthy, as He did the brother of Jared. He wants us to be willing to come unto Him, to obey His command, to seek Him out, and to approach Him as best we can. If we do this, He will make us worthy.

This willingness is portrayed very visually in the law of Moses. There were many offerings that each Israelite was commanded to make. These offerings were a way of approaching God—a way of seeking communion, covenant, and oneness with Him. Many were too poor to possess the necessary goods for the prescribed offerings, yet God always made provision for the poor. If they could not afford the ideal offering, they could bring something else. For example, in Leviticus 5, the Lord describes many kinds of sins that would estrange someone from God. These things made one ritually (and, symbolically, spiritually) unclean, cutting one off from communion with God through ritual and social life (and, symbolically, spiritually). In order to overcome the effects of these various sins, a trespass offering had to be made: "And it shall be, when He shall be guilty in one of these *things,* that He shall confess that He hath sinned in that *thing:* And He shall bring His trespass offering unto the Lord for His sin which He hath sinned, a female from the flock, a lamb or a kid of the goats, for a sin offering; and the priest shall make an Atonement for Him concerning His sin" (Lev. 5:5–6).

Such an offering was the ideal situation. Yet a lamb or goat was more than many could afford. So the Lord stipulated that "if He be not able to bring a lamb, then He shall bring for His trespass, which He hath committed, two turtledoves, or two young pigeons, unto the LORD; one for a sin offering, and the other for a burnt offering" (Lev. 5:7). For some, even doves were too expensive. Allowance was made for this as well: "If He be not able to bring two turtledoves, or two young pigeons, then He that sinned shall bring for His offering the tenth part of an ephah of fine flour for a sin offering" (Lev. 5:11).

There was a practical side to these provisos. No one was to be left out of the religious life of Israel, no matter his economic abilities.

But one spiritual symbol that is even more meaningful lies behind the allowances made in the offerings of the poor. If these offerings symbolize our ability to approach God—and they do—then we can see what God does with those who have less to offer Him. Some may have great spiritual gifts, talents, opportunities, time, and means to offer to God. Others have less. It does not matter, because God expects and accepts what we have.

In terms of our own worthiness, spiritual state, and abilities, we each have differing degrees. We will even have variations within our own lifetime. There are times I feel as if I am doing pretty well, as if I can approach God more easily. Then there are times when I have reminded myself in stark ways of my fallen nature and ungodly character; at these times I feel I have very little to offer God—I feel as if I cannot come unto God because I am too spiritually poor. But God does not feel this way about the matter. If I do not have a spiritual lamb to offer, I can bring a spiritual dove. If I don't have even that, I can bring spiritual flour. God accepts whatever I have—or whoever I am. Just as He did not tell the Israelite who had only flour to stay away from the altar, He does not tell us when we feel spiritually bankrupt that we cannot come unto Him. Instead, He tells us to bring what we have; it is good enough. In our moments of spiritual destitution, we should remember that the Lord said, "Blessed are the poor in spirit who come unto me, for theirs is the kingdom of heaven" (3 Ne. 12:3). He did not say that there was a problem with being poor in spirit (we all are), but rather that when we are poor we should come unto Him, for then He can and will reward us with the kingdom of heaven. Not a bad tradeoff. One lesson of the flour offering is that whatever my spiritual state, it is good enough to allow me to approach God, if I am just willing to approach.

This is powerfully taught in another place in the Mosaic Law. One of the greatest symbols of God's salvation was the Passover. Here the Israelites celebrated how God spared them from death because of the blood of a sacrificial lamb. Few things hold more powerful and pertinent symbols of our salvation through Christ than this ritual. But a few symbols are often overlooked. One is that if a family were too little (I suppose in numbers or resources), they were to be taken in with another family so that they too could partake of the symbolic salvation (see Ex. 12:4). Similarly, while typically being ritually unclean prevented an Israelite from taking part in religious rituals, this was not true of the Passover. The Lord specifically revealed to Moses that even those who were unclean could and should take part in this ritual precursor of the Atonement (see Num. 9:6–14). In fact, the only people who were in trouble with the Passover were those who could, but did not, partake of it.

Think of the symbolism. Your (spiritual) size and (spiritual) resources do not matter to the Lord; He will extend the protective Passover to all. Your state of cleanliness does not alter your ability to partake of saving grace; God will pass (spiritual) death over for all those who are willing to come unto Him through this ritual. It is not what someone had to offer, nor their state at the time of the offering, that was important to God as He symbolically saved Israel. It was whether or not they were willing to come. And so it is with you and I. Forget how clean and able you feel; just come unto God. When you are seeking salvation, He will start with you wherever you are. However small you are, however unclean you are, if you will take advantage of the blood of the Lamb, God will honor that blood and cause (spiritual) death to pass you by. Just come.

Working with Our Doubts and Weaknesses

Remember that the Savior's mission is to help those who cannot help themselves. Furthermore, remember that this describes all of us; none of us can overcome on our own. Thus we can be assured that He will help us through our doubts, fears, foibles, and weaknesses. We can see this repeatedly in the scriptures. In order to demonstrate the point, we will look at two of the greatest prophets of all time, both of them leaders of dispensations.

The Lord called Enoch to the ministry despite whatever shortcomings Enoch had. When the Lord first told Enoch to begin to prophesy, Enoch's response was to bow to the earth and say, "Why is it that I have found favor in thy sight, and am but a lad, and all the people hate me; for I am slow of speech; wherefore am I thy servant?" (Moses 6:31).

Does this sound like a great prophet, full of faith and eager to serve the Lord? To me, it sounds like a humble servant who feels there are others who would be better qualified than he is. He is painfully aware that he is young, unpopular, and doesn't speak well. From Enoch's point of view there must surely have been others who could do the work better. He probably thought to himself that the Lord just didn't know about his shortcomings the way he knew about them; surely the Lord wouldn't appoint him to this task if he knew all about Enoch's problems and inabilities.

In this, Enoch was wrong. Undoubtedly the Lord knew all about Enoch. He also knew what Enoch could become with the Lord's help. Enoch's native abilities. Nothing else mattered—not his past, not his relationships with others, not any of it. What did matter was that the Lord could do great things with and through Enoch. Note how the Lord's response does two things. It reminds Enoch of God's ability to make of him something greater than what Enoch believed he could be. It also points out the foolishness of Enoch presuming that he knew better than God what he could do with the Lord's help. Here's how the Lord responded: "Go forth and do as I have commanded thee, and no man shall pierce thee. Open thy mouth, and it shall be filled, and I will give thee utterance, for all flesh is in my hands, and I will do as seemeth me good" (Moses 6:32).

What a poignant reminder for all of us. Whatever problems we have, or whatever problems we have created for ourselves, are puny in comparison to God's love for us and His power to change us. He can make slow-of-speech Enoch someone who cannot be pierced and whose mouth is filled. And why can He do this? Because He has power over all men. Because He really knows what is best, so He will do what seems best to Him. The phrase *for all flesh is in my hands* means that we are included. We are in God's hands; He can do with us what seems good to Him (thank goodness He loves us). This means that whatever our problems or doubts, He can make something great out of us, just as He did with Enoch.

Moses was very similar to Enoch when the Lord called him. This great prophet was slow in being assured by the Lord and believing that the Lord really could make of him all He was saying He would. When Moses was first told the Lord would use him to deliver Israel, Moses said, "Who am I, that I should go unto Pharaoh, and that I should bring forth the children of Israel out of Egypt?" (Ex. 3:11).

The Lord reassured Moses and gave him a sign. Moses immediately brought up a complication, telling the Lord that he didn't even know how to introduce the Lord to the Israelites (see Ex. 3:13). The Lord answered this question and then instructed Moses further. Moses then said, "But behold, they will not believe me, nor hearken unto my voice" (Ex. 4:1). In order to reassure Moses, the Lord showed several miracles He would work through Moses. Finally Moses plead, "O my Lord, I am not eloquent, neither heretofore, nor since thou has spoken unto thy servant: but I am slow of speech and of a slow tongue" (Ex. 4:10).

Here Moses seems to be saying not only that he has always had this problem, but also that it hadn't improved since the Lord had called him (only moments before). The Lord worked with Moses in his doubts, demonstrating the foolishness of his concerns and the greatness of God's power, just as He had with Enoch. He replied, "Who hath made man's mouth? Or who maketh the dumb, or deaf, or the seeing, or the blind? Have not I the Lord? Now therefore go, and I will be with thy mouth, and teach thee what thou shalt say" (Ex. 4:11–12). In effect, the Lord reminded Moses that while he may have had fears about a particular faculty or quality, God was the creator of our faculties and could certainly enhance them. Even after all this, Moses was worried about his abilities, so God gave him Aaron as a spokesman.

I suspect Moses was not so different than many of us. He had problems, and he had fears and doubts born of those problems. The Lord was more than able to lift Moses to a higher plane, to help him overcome those problems. Yet Moses doubted. The Lord worked with him, and Moses doubted again. The Lord worked with him *again*, and Moses doubted *again*. And so it continued, over and over. This helps us see that while our continual struggles may be tiresome, the Lord will not tire of helping us. I believe that if Moses had doubted five more times, the Lord would have helped him five more times. The point is that whatever our state, whatever our problems, the Lord stands ready to work with us as much as is necessary to bring us to a higher state.

What we must realize is that the Lord does not expect us to have enough or be enough. It really doesn't matter how much we lack, He has enough to make up the difference. Whatever we can bring to the table is enough. We just have to bring what we are, in whatever form we may be. The Lord is able to make our pittance into whatever it needs to be.

This is demonstrated so visibly in the miracle of feeding the five thousand. The Savior saw the need to feed the multitude and asked His disciples what they use for food. All the disciples could find was a boy with five barley loaves and two small fishes. From a mortal perspective, Andrew was right to ask, "what are they among so many?" (John 6:9). From a mortal perspective, of course, this tiny offering could do nothing for the multitude. From God's perspective, all they had to do was bring what they had. He had the ability to make it enough. After the five thousand had been fed, there were twelve baskets of bread left over.

While this is an inspiring miracle, I think it pales in comparison with how this principle works in our own lives. Because He loves us, God wants to make so much of us. It doesn't matter at all what we already are. Just bring your pitiful self to Him, and He will make you what you need to be. Because of all the problems we have, all the things we've done, all the bad qualities we have developed, it may seem like what we are won't be good enough. But just as the five loaves and two fishes were made into enough, your poor, flawed character will be turned into something more godly than you have ever dreamed of—if you will just bring it as an offering to God.

Elder Jeffrey R. Holland spoke of this when he said that we shouldn't worry about the Savior running out of the ability to help us or anyone else. The miracle of feeding the five thousands demonstrated powerfully that His grace is sufficient.[24] However ungodly you are, God and His Son can make up the difference.

What we need to come to understand is that whatever we are, whatever we have, whatever we can do will never be close to enough. On our own we can never, ever merit what God wants to give us. "Since man had fallen, He could not merit anything of himself" (Alma 22:14). Thus we must instead rely "alone upon the merits of Christ, who was the author and the finisher of their faith" (Moro. 6:4). Fortunately, Christ has merit enough, no matter how large the deficit between what we need to be and what we are.

Stated differently, let us consider a great prize available to you and to me if each of us had only one hundred million dollars. If you could bring ten thousand dollars and I could bring one thousand dollars, we would both be far short of what we need. If we were to ever receive the prize it would be because someone else stepped in and paid the difference. To you and me the difference between ten thousand dollars and one thousand dollars is great. But to someone who will pay millions for both of us, the difference between what we bring with us is negligible. It does not matter. He only asks that we bring what we have. He will make up whatever difference there is. He has merit enough. All He asks is that you bring what you have or what you are. The key is not what we bring to Him, but that we bring ourselves to Him.

This same lesson was taught in a similar way in the book of Judges. There the Israelites were being oppressed by the Midianites. God raised up a judge, one who did not seem to possess the natural abilities to lead Israel out of bondage. Gideon was described as a man of valor, but like Moses and Enoch he knew his shortcomings. When called, he protested that "my family is poor in Manasseh, and I am the least in my father's house" (Judg. 6:15). The Lord assured Gideon that He could make him a deliverer. Gideon still needed assurance, and sought a sign from the Lord. The Lord assuaged Gideon's doubts and miraculously consumed an offering with fire. Upon receiving the assurance he desired, Gideon set about the Lord's work. Twice more along the way he would want assurance from the Lord that he was truly up to the task with the Lord's help, and twice more the Lord complied and sent signs to reassure Gideon.

Gideon raised a large army. In this case the Lord wanted Israel to know that it was not by their might that they would be freed from Midianite oppression. Twice the Lord reduced the army, until Gideon went forth to face the armies of Midian with only three hundred men. With this paltry force the Midianites were miraculously routed, and Israel found freedom for a time.

Clearly the Lord wanted Israel to have no opportunity to mistake who had delivered them. He reduced the army "lest Israel vaunt themselves against me, saying mine own hand hath saved me" (Judg. 7:2). This is a real event. Yet I also believe that the story happened and is recorded in a way that we can see an application in our own lives.

Similarly, think of how Jonathan and his armor bearer routed an entire Philistine garrison because they knew that "there is no restraint to the Lord to save by many or by few" (1 Sam. 14:5). Bolstered by this faith-filled perspective, the two of them attacked a fortress and, with the help of the Lord, conquered. If the Lord can conquer an entire army with least-important Gideon and only three hundred Israelites, what can He do with me? If two Israelites accompanied by the strength of the Lord can route a fortress, surely He can make me enough to conquer all that is before me. It does not matter how weak I am in comparison with the struggles that lie ahead, it is irrelevant how frequently I fail as I try to overcome the natural man inside. God is powerful enough to make up the difference. He can help me to miraculously route the enemies of my soul, including myself as my own worst enemy.

CHAPTER SIX
FAITH AND EFFORT
TO THE END

And He said, I will not let thee go, except thou bless me. . . .
And He blessed Him there.
(Gen. 32:26–29)

Did You Expect to Finish?

We teach that with God's help we can conquer anything, and this is true. But we also need to know that we won't conquer everything before we die. We will never reach a point in life when we are coasting, when we have sufficiently battled our own imprudence, impatience, vanity, pride, jealousy, covetousness, and all manner of ungodliness. In this life we will not rid ourselves of these things so much that we no longer have to struggle.

We *always* need to be striving and struggling with something. Take Nephi as an example. Seemingly right up to the end of his life he felt he needed to struggle with "droop[ing] in sin" and with not giving place for "the enemy of my soul" (2 Ne. 4:28). As I read Nephi's laments, it seems to me he is concerned with becoming angry when his brethren want to kill him or his family. I must admit I am not at this spiritual plane. I think I would feel justified in being angry with someone who was trying to kill my family. But for Nephi, this was something he was working on even toward the end of his life, and seems to have been for some time. If Nephi continued to "give way to temptations" (2 Ne. 4:27), perhaps we should not feel bad if we also have to keep working on the same things throughout our lives.

Can you imagine God not expecting us to struggle right up to the day we die? Can you picture Him not wanting us to be trying to overcome right up to the end? Yet we get down when we haven't conquered something—when we have to keep working on it, as if we should be able to rid ourselves of this particular problem and all others. Maybe one day you will conquer—with the Savior's help—the particular thing you are most vexed with right now. But then you will find some other element of your character with which you need to struggle. However, it is quite likely that you will have to struggle for the rest of your mortal probation with the problem that frustrates you most for the rest of your life.

Both the Atonement and our own effort are necessary for progress, but the struggle may last a literal lifetime. Some thorns never leave our sides; they remain throughout our mortal existence as we grow stronger in the struggle. As Elder D. Todd Christofferson said, real change and repentance require us to constantly strive and change, but we can find something holy in that kind of striving.[25]

Thus, at times the whole point may be that we continue to struggle despite how difficult it is. Remember Jacob. When he desperately prayed to the Lord that he and his family would be spared from the wrath of his estranged brother Esau, an angel appeared to him. The blessing he sought did not come immediately. Instead, Jacob wrestled with that angel until the morning broke. All night long he struggled and wrestled, never giving up. And when the dawn came, it almost seemed like the angel cheated. He put Jacob's leg out of joint. But that did not stop Jacob. Though he must have been exhausted, and though he could only limp on a painful leg, he *would not let go!* No matter how hard and long the night had been, no matter how difficult it was for him to move, no matter how painful the experience, he was not going to give up. He struggled right to the end—and at the end he received both what he had asked and a blessing greater than the one for which he had sought. In the end, it does not seem to be Jacob's ability to beat his opponent that mattered—it was that he would continue the struggle right up to the end, even if he lost the battle.

Jacob's life as a whole serves as a lesson in struggling to the end. Though he was one of the greatest prophets, his life was an unending series of difficulties. He was not his father's favorite son. This was so true that, though the Lord had promised he would gain the birthright, Isaac intended to bestow it upon Jacob's brother Esau. Rebekah and Jacob had to resort to subterfuge to get Isaac to give Jacob the promised blessing. Apparently when Isaac discovered this, he must have realized that his wife (as is so often the case) had helped him do what he should have done in the first place.

However, Jacob's obtaining of the blessing did not make his life easy. Instead, he had to flee in order to escape his brother's wrath. As a result, he would spend much of his life in exile, away from his family. Fortunately, in this exile he found his extended family—and, most importantly a girl he deeply loved. After working for seven years to earn the right to marry her, he found he had been tricked and had married the wrong girl. He then had to work another seven years to obtain his true love.

Jacob worked many more years for his father-in-law, who changed his wages ten times as he tried to prevent Jacob from receiving blessings from the Lord. In the midst of this, Jacob and his wives went through the most difficult of family situations, dealing with jealousies and strife within the family. Finally the Lord told Jacob to return to his homeland. Though Jacob thought that his family might die as a result, he obeyed the Lord. It was during this return that he wrestled with the angel.

Upon his return to Canaan, Jacob learned that his brother was no longer angry with him, and they reconciled. But this did not mark the end of Jacob's troubles. His sons had strife amongst themselves and with others. His daughter was raped, his sons wrought a horrible revenge, and Jacob had to deal with the repercussions. The fighting among his sons was so great that nine of them actually wanted to kill another, but ended up selling him into slavery instead. While he did not know the true details of how Joseph was lost from the family, Jacob's heart was truly broken by the loss of his beloved wife to death during childbirth and then by the loss of Joseph. Jacob later temporarily lost one of his other sons to prison in Egypt and was paralyzed by the fear of also losing his youngest son. Despite all these difficulties, Jacob continued to serve the Lord and to try to bring his family to Him. Just as he had with the angel, Jacob held on through all these great trials. And just as what happened when wrestling the angel, eventually Jacob received the blessings he had wanted with all his heart. In his very old age he made the difficult trip to Egypt, was reunited with his beloved Joseph, and met grandchildren he never knew he had. He lived the rest of his days in a measure of prosperity with his family reconciled and together. These blessings only came after a long lifetime of struggle. Jacob wrestled to the very end, when he was finally blessed by God with the great desire of his heart.

If Jacob struggled with various things to the end, should we expect to do less? Jacob's difficult life serves as a metaphor for the many things we will struggle and wrestle with in our own lives. Some of our strivings will be with family matters, or great loss, or with difficult tasks. But surely one of the things we will have to wrestle with until the very end is our own propensity for folly.

While I hesitate to use a wicked person as an example, I do think there is something to be learned from the terrible leader Shiz, whose story we read in the book of Ether. Even after Coriantumr beheaded him, Shiz rose up on his hands and struggled for breath. I do not believe that to receive salvation we need to have overcome all of our proclivities for ungodliness before we die. No one but the Savior will. But I do believe that right up until our death we should be striving to overcome them. Even on my deathbed I hope to rise up on my hands one last time in a struggle to overcome pride, laziness, or whatever my greatest difficulty is at that point. I will spend my entire life fighting the natural man within me, but I know I won't have beaten him when I die.

Even though I will not have conquered at that point, as long as I am still trying, whatever I have done will be enough. It will be my five loaves and two fishes, my three-hundred-man army. The Lord will make up the rest. He will not abandon me; because I am still struggling, He will accept the offering of the struggle. His love and power are enough to conquer the enemy for me.

There is a tension between concepts here that we must delicately balance. We must always remember that the power of the Atonement is enough to change any aspect of every one of us. This is real, and it really happens in our lives. Yet at the same time there are some things that the Lord will ask us to struggle with for a long time, perhaps all our lives, before that change comes or before it fully comes. As Elder D. Todd Christofferson explained, we would mock the Savior's suffering during His Atonement if we expected Him to change us completely with absolutely no effort on our part; instead, we ask Him to change us as a reward for our most faithful and determined efforts (see 2 Ne. 25:23). Even more than praying for His mercy, we might pray for the opportunity and time to strive and overcome what we can.[26] While our emphasis needs to be on the power of the Atonement to make those changes, we should not be surprised, downhearted, or discouraged that oft times we struggle for a literal lifetime with some things. In fact, we should be grateful that we have the time to continue the effort.

In the midst of struggling with some aspects of your nature, the Lord might help you to have sudden, born-again experiences after which you will have overcome those aspects. Perhaps one day you find the ability to forgive someone you have never been able to forgive or to love someone you have never been able to love. There will be other parts of your nature that you will struggle with for years that the Lord will change gradually, almost imperceptibly, over the course of a lifetime, helping you bit by bit as you struggle on your own. Perhaps He will help you to gradually become more slow to anger, helping you just a little at a time to develop the ability to control your temper. There will be yet another side of you that the Lord will help you change only in the next life. For example, He may help you stop a pornographic habit, but you might have to fight against the desire to give in to this sin for your entire life. While the Lord may have made you into a creature that could stop viewing such filth, you might not have stop desiring it until you have passed on to the next life. From time to time you might even give in, only to start the process of forsaking it all over again. Most will battle against pride throughout mortal probation. Many will fight to control anger for as long as they live. You might be someone who struggles with avoiding gossip for your whole life, going through spurts of successes and failures in your struggle with this, or any other, vice.

The point is that in whatever ways we and the Lord may have conquered something in our lives, we should not expect that we will ever be completely through with the wrestle against the fallen nature that comprises our mortal probation. We will discuss grace and effort in more detail below—but we must be very aware that every aspect of being saved by grace, including being saved from various sins with which we struggle, will happen in God's own good time, according to His all-knowing and benevolent will. If we forget this, we are likely to see our struggles as signs of our failure rather than signs of our continued march through mortal probation. Such forgetfulness will surely lead us to feelings of hopelessness and despair.

We should not allow Satan to lead us to despair or to depressed feelings when we have not conquered. When these feelings come we should behave like Jacob, who, even when the angel dislocated his thigh, held on all the harder, determined he would not give up until he received the blessing he desired. While we should never be satisfied with our progress, we can be satisfied with our continuation of the struggle. We can be satisfied with the fact that even when it feels as if life, Satan, and our own silliness have cut our head off, we will still raise up on our hands and try to conquer our enemy. Let's just make sure we have chosen the right enemy—that we are struggling against ungodliness. Then God will help us conquer all, conquer the enemy of our souls, even conquer death and hell.

But don't become disheartened or faint because you continue to struggle. The fact that you are struggling still, trying to beat the same old sins and shortcomings, does not mean that there is something wrong or hopeless about you. It means that you are still progressing. Because God loves you He will help you progress beyond your own abilities, both in this life and in the next. We *will* fail. He *will not*.

I already recognize weaknesses in some of my children that I believe they will still be working on when they leave my house. They will probably strive with these things their entire lives. Does it make me love them less? No. I love them all the more as I see them struggle, fail, feel terrible about failing, struggle, do better, and then fail again. I love them regardless—nothing will change that. But I think my love for them deepens as I watch them try so hard, even after periods of giving up.

In the same way, I am convinced God loves each one of us regardless of our repeated failures. I am certain He stands ready to take us back again. I am convinced of the truth that whenever we try again He will anxiously help us—in the way that is best for us. He loves us and has covenanted with us. Whenever you reach out to Him and "have him as your God" (Gen. 17:6–7), He will have you as His child. He will bring you home. It is what He and our great Redeemer do.

Helping us with tasks that are too great for us is a major theme of the Old Testament. Think of the tasks set before Israel. First, they had to escape bondage from the superpower of their day—Egypt. This would be impossible for them to do on their own, but God did it for them. They then needed to conquer the giant, fortified cities and equipped armies of the promised land. The Israelites were correct in their assessment that this was too great a task for them (see Num. 14). But it was not impossible with the help of God. As God sent Joshua into the promised land to conquer, He repeatedly told Joshua, "Be strong and of a good courage" (Josh. 1:6, 7, 9, 18). He assured Joshua that He would not forsake him. With God's help they did conquer. As the Lord Himself put it, "the Lord hath redeemed Jacob, and ransomed him from the hand of him that was stronger than he" (Jer. 31:11). In order to help the Israelites overcome these large people and great walls, the Lord took down some walls (see Josh. 6), enticed enemy armies out of their walled cities and then miraculously prolonged the day of battle (see Josh. 10), or gave Israel tactical directions and aid in battle (see Josh. 8).

Time and again the Lord helped Israel overcome obstacles too great for them except when they failed to turn to the Lord. The powerful lesson taught in the sweeping events of Israel's past is that our small ability to overcome does not matter—God has power enough.

The Need to Believe

As we deal with our ongoing exertions and our inabilities to win those struggles, the key is that we must turn to the Lord and we must believe. Sometimes we focus so much on our own lack of ability, or on our own repeated failures that have estranged us from God, that we fail to believe He can really exalt us. In contrast, we need to accept the stark truth: if we are willing, God is able.

Perhaps God's delivering ability and the problems that stem from our doubts are illustrated best in the Old Testament. Within its pages we find *the great* scriptural story of deliverance: the Exodus. In particular we want to look at the wilderness experience of the Exodus, because symbolically it is where we can locate ourselves.[27]

We understand the full import of Israel's meandering travels best when we remember that their journey, while a real event, serves as a symbol of our mortal journey. Just as we are in bondage to sin and our natural man, Israel was in bondage to Egypt. They turned their backs on this symbol of sin and the world through a baptism-like experience in the Red Sea,and embarked into the wilderness. Scriptural wildernesses generally symbolize our mortal probation (see Alma 17:9; Ether 6:4–7; and 1 Ne. 8).[28]

Soon after entering the wilderness, Israel made a covenant at Sinai in a temple-like setting. After years of wandering, they were eventually brought to the River Jordan (symbolic of the veil) and crossed it, entering the promised land (symbolic of the true promised land, the celestial kingdom). What happens to Israel in this story is indicative of the pattern of our lives.

While Israel had plenty of problems in the wilderness, two incidents—the very events that forced them to receive the lower law and wander in the wilderness—demonstrate their general problem. That problem was a lack of faith in the delivering power of Jehovah.

The first incident happened at Mount Sinai. By now Israel had seen brilliant displays of God's delivering power. God had shown them His mighty hand through the plagues, including the destroying angel. He had sent fire and parted the sea to save them from the most powerful army on earth. They had thus far survived the desert by means of miraculously supplied water, quail, and manna. The Lord had defeated the Amalekites for them. After all this, He brought them to the Holy Mount to bring them unto Himself.

There God commanded Israel to prepare themselves, "for the third day the Lord will come down in the sight of all the people upon mount Sinai" (Ex. 19:11). Israel obediently sanctified themselves for three days. Then Moses "brought forth the people out of the camp to meet with God" (Ex. 19:16–17). Thunder, lighting, and the sound of trumpets emanated from the mountain as it was enveloped in a thick cloud and began to quake. Then the people heard the voice of the Lord; they all heard Him as He dictated the Ten Commandments (see Ex. 19:18–19 and Deut. 5:22–25).

Apparently all of this was overwhelming for Israel. Though the Lord was ready to reveal Himself to each one of them, the Israelites sent their leaders to Moses:

> And it came to pass, when ye heard the voice out of the midst of the darkness, (for the mountain did burn with fire,) that ye came near unto me, even all the heads of your tribes, and your elders;
>
> And ye said, Behold, the Lord our God hath shewed us His glory and His greatness, and we have heard His voice out of the midst of the fire: we have seen this day that God doth talk with man, and He liveth.
>
> Now therefore why should we die? for this great fire will consume us: if we hear the voice of the Lord our God any more, then we shall die.
>
> For who is there of all flesh, that hath heard the voice of the living God speaking out of the midst of the fire, as we have, and lived?
>
> Go thou near, and hear all that the Lord our God shall say: and speak thou unto us all that the Lord our God shall speak unto thee; and we will hear it, and do it. (Deut. 5:23–27)

Even though Moses told them to "fear not" (Ex. 20:20), "the people stood afar off, and Moses drew near unto the thick darkness where God was" (Ex. 20:21). They refused to go up and meet the Lord themselves. They were afraid that if they came into the presence of God they would die.

Remember, Israel vividly knew firsthand of God's delivering power. Yet even with all this, they refused to come into the presence of the Lord. In short, *they did not believe* that the Lord had power to deliver them safely into His own consuming presence. Moses' words "fear not" should have served as a forceful reminder of God's delivering power, because those were the same words He had spoken at the Red Sea when God had provided one of their most spectacular and visible deliverances (see Ex. 14:13). Yet even this did not bolster Israel's faith, and they went "afar off."

Joseph Smith taught that this was the great downfall of Israel. He said, "When God offers a blessing or knowledge to a man and He refuses to receive it, He will be damned. [Such is] the case of the Israelites praying that God would speak to Moses and not to them, in consequence of which He cursed them with a carnal law."[29] It is disheartening to realize that Israel served for thousands of years under

a lower law because they did not believe that the Lord had the power
to bring them to "meet with God" and live.

This same lack of faith surfaced again when the children of Israel
arrived at the borders of the promised land in Kadesh-Barnea. Moses
poignantly reminded Israel of God's promise to give them the land
when they arrived at the oasis: "ye are come unto the mountain of
the Amorites, which the Lord our God doth give unto us. Behold,
the Lord thy God hath set the land before thee: go up and possess it,
as the Lord God of thy fathers hath said unto thee; fear not, neither
be discouraged" (Deut. 1:20–21). Again Moses used the same words
pronounced in the dramatic deliverance at the Red Sea: "fear not."

With this injunction, under Moses' leadership, Israel sent one
spy from each tribe to learn about the promised land and what they
must do to inherit it (see Deut. 1:22 and Num. 14:1). All of the spies
reported that the land was beautiful and fertile, an ideal place to live.
Only Joshua and Caleb urged them to actually go into this fabled
countryside. The other spies feared the cities and men they saw within
Canaan.

Years later, Moses reported that the people

> would not go up, but rebelled against the commandment of
> the Lord your God:
> And ye murmured in your tents, and said, Because the
> Lord hated us, He hath brought us forth out of the land
> of Egypt, to deliver us into the hand of the Amorites, to
> destroy us.
> Whither shall we go up? Our brethren have discouraged
> our heart, saying, The people is greater and taller than we;
> the cities are great and walled up to heaven; and moreover
> we have seen the sons of the Anakims [giants] there. (Deut.
> 1:26–28)

Once again Moses emphasized that Israel did not believe the Lord
could deliver them from their enemies and bring them safely into the
promised land. Though they had seen one of the mightiest armies on
earth, that of Egypt—which in comparison must have made the Amorites
look weak—defeated and destroyed by the hand of the Lord, they were
afraid that He could not bring them into His rest in the promised land.

Moses tried to stir up their faith by reminding them of the amazing power the Lord had used in their behalf before: "and in the wilderness, where thou hast seen how that the Lord thy God bare thee, as a man doth bear His son, in all the way that ye went, until ye came into this place" (Deut. 1:31). Still, the Israelites would not go, causing Moses to lament, "yet in this thing ye did not *believe* the Lord your God" (Deut. 1:32; emphasis added).

The Lord asked Moses, "how long will this people provoke me? And how long will it be ere they *believe* me, for all the signs which I have shewed among them?" (Num. 14:11; emphasis added). Here the Lord highlighted Israel's problem as a lack of belief in His promise to give them the promised land. Though they knew the Lord had great delivering power, they just couldn't get themselves to see how He could overcome these particular obstacles. As a result, the Lord swore that no one from that generation would enter the promised land (see Deut. 1:35). Because of their refusal and inability to believe that the Lord could deliver them, the Israelites waited forty years before receiving their inheritance.

As with the rest of the Old Testament, we should apply what happened to Israel in this story to our own lives as Israelite individuals. The story reveals what is sure to be one of our greatest obstacles in our attempts to return to the Lord. That obstacle must be our own inability to think that the Lord can actually deliver us given our own circumstances, inabilities, foibles, and weaknesses. When we overinflate our own aptitude for messing up and simultaneously fail to have faith in His delivering power, it could keep us from the celestial kingdom. It could prevent God from helping us return to Him.

It seems that many of us believe strongly in many things about the gospel, yet we struggle with its very core: the truth that Christ can deliver us and bring us into His promised land. It is easy to believe that He can and will save others but not us.

Just as Israel had seen God deliver them in the past, you and I may very well understand that Christ suffered for us all and made it possible for us to repent. But at the same time we may not feel that *our specific selves* can be exalted. We know ourselves and our backsliding too well. Simply put, such an attitude is a lack of faith in the atoning power of Christ.[30] Though we may have many times felt the redeeming and delivering power of Christ's Atonement, we sometimes wonder if it can really fundamentally change us. You and I may have repented and felt the cleansing and delivering power of Christ when a small and momentary measure of peace came into our lives, signaling forgiveness. Truly, deliverance from one sin is an ample demonstration of the Lord's delivering power. The cleansing we have felt in our lives is much like Israel's being delivered from the Egyptians. Since we have been forgiven in the past, could not the Lord deliver us from all of our sins, shortcomings, stupidities, and foibles and bring us into the celestial kingdom? We may as well ask why, after having defeated the Egyptian army, could not the Lord defeat the Amorites and the Anakim in the promised land? The answer is the same: of course He can.

Did the Israelites have legitimate fears? Yes. Do we? Yes. At Sinai the Israelites feared that coming before the Lord in an unworthy state would prove their destruction. This is a reasonable fear, since no unclean thing can survive the presence of the Lord (see 1 Ne. 15:34). Being unclean leads mankind to the twin monsters of death and hell (see 2 Ne. 9:10, 19; Alma 5:7–10). The Amorites and the Anakim of the promised land are the perfect symbols for death and hell. These people were two obstacles that the children of Israel could not have overcome on their own and that would have prevented them from inheriting the promised land.

Death and hell are to us what the Amorites and Anakim were to ancient Israel. These are obstacles that, no matter what we do or how hard we try, we will never overcome on our own. We must rely on the Lord to deliver us from them. But so often when we see our fallen natures we think it is something that either we must overcome or that is beyond the power of anyone to overcome. Both ways of thinking are wrong. They are just our own versions of the Amorites and the Anakim. The Lord can just as easily deliver us as He did ancient Israel. The obstacles are not the issue—the issue is our acceptance of His delivering power. Just as surely as large people and large walls were not too great an obstacle for the Lord, our own fallen foibles are no match for His delivering power.

While it was true that the Israelites could not have withstood the presence of the Lord without His help, it was perfectly clear that the Lord could safely bring them before Him as He had done with Moses. And while the Israelites could not conquer the Amorites and the Anakim without the Lord, it was abundantly clear that they *could* conquer them with His help. They had ample evidence of this. But they still refused to believe. For latter-day Israel, the important thing is that the atoning powers of Christ can overcome our uncleanness— it can conquer all those aspects of ourselves we worry about. Our choice, like ancient Israel, is whether or not we will believe in the Lord's delivering power. Will we "fear not," or will we give in to our own doubts about our future? Will we see only the Amorites (our own weaknesses)? Or will we remember how our own shortcomings pale in comparison to Christ's atoning power?

How to Believe

For ancient Israel, Kadesh-barnea could not be the end. They had entered into a covenant with the Lord, and as a part of that covenant they *would* inherit the promised land. But first the Lord had to punish them with a purpose. He would strip them of all unbelievers, meaning that none of the adults who had refused to go into the promised land would be alive when Israel did receive their inheritance. Thus, Israel was forced to remain in the wilderness, a place where they had no chance of survival except by depending on the Lord. This experience created a generation raised in complete reliance on the Lord.[31] In other words, the Lord tore them down so He could build them up. He wiped away their unbelief by purging them in the wilderness in such a way that they became accustomed to relying on His delivering power. The process took forty years. But because of His love and His covenant, the Lord did not give up on Israel.

We, too, are in a covenant with our loving God. As members of the covenant, the Lord will give each of us the wilderness/mortal probation experiences we all need in order to develop true faith in the atoning power of Christ. Much of that refining experience may very well be an unending struggle with the same sins and problems. The point is not our ability to rid ourselves of these things but rather our ability to believe that God can. Just as ancient Israel had to be stripped of all her unbelievers, we have to strip ourselves of all unbelief. If we choose to do this, the Lord will bring us to the point where we believe enough in His delivering power that He will be able to deliver us. We must remember that this deliverance will not come in this life. Part of the Lord's covenant with ancient Israel was that they would inherit the promised land. Likewise, part of His covenant with each member of modern Israel is that we may receive the inheritance of eternal life. Eventually.

Because we are so familiar with the many ungodly aspects of our nature, it is difficult to believe that we will inherit all that the Father has. But continued reliance on Him will help us see with an eye of faith that He has the ability to bring us to this inheritance. Just as He delivered Israel from bondage, Egyptian armies, starvation, and Amorites, He can deliver us from sin, the forces of Satan, and even our own fallen natures. He has the power to justify and sanctify us. His Atonement can change our natures and make us new creatures in Christ—in other words, Christ-like creatures. It is difficult to imagine ourselves thus, so it is hard to believe in this power. However, just as Israel finally entered the promised land, we can finally inherit the celestial kingdom and exaltation. We must learn to say, "Our fathers trusted in thee: they trusted, and thou didst deliver them. They cried unto thee, and were delivered: they trusted in thee, and were not confounded" (Ps. 22:4–5). Along with that, we must also see how that deliverance applies to us.

Eventually, a generation that fully believed the Lord could deliver them came again to the borders of the promised land. This time they did so at the River Jordan. As they prepared to cross over this division between them and the promised land—highly symbolic of that which separates us from God— the Lord gave them explicit instructions through Joshua. It was only by demonstrating both faith and obedience that they entered into the land of their inheritance.

As their fathers had done at Sinai, Israel spent the day sanctifying themselves. They gathered their tents and belongings and arranged themselves behind the priests who bore the Ark of the Covenant. The lid of the Ark of the Covenant was called the "mercy seat," or "seat of atonement." There was no more poignant symbol of Christ and His delivering power than the Ark of the Covenant. Only by following this symbol could Israel enter into the promised land.

Upon Joshua's command, the priests carried the ark and marched toward the River Jordan. Israel followed. They had been promised that they would reach the other side, but they first had to demonstrate their faith. They marched up to and then *into* the river. It was not until the feet of the priests bearing the Ark were in the waters of the river that the Lord exerted His delivering powers and parted the water. "And the priests that bare the ark of the covenant of the Lord stood firm on dry ground in the midst of Jordan, and all the Israelites passed over on dry ground, until all the people were passed clean over Jordan" (Josh. 3:17). After this demonstration of faith, following squarely behind the seat of atonement and trusting fully in the delivering power of Him whom it symbolized, Israel finally entered its land of inheritance.

So it is with us. As we demonstrate our faith in Christ's delivering power, even to the point of getting our feet wet, the Lord will part the veil and bring about our redemption. In all this, the vital lesson we must learn from our Israelite ancestors is that no matter how difficult it may seem, we need to have full faith in the delivering power of our Lord and Savior. God loves us and has the power to deliver us no matter how often we mess up. Of this we must become convinced deep within our hearts. It is crucial to fully believe that if we are willing, God is able.

CHAPTER SEVEN
WHAT WE CAN BECOME

Hide thy face from my sins, and blot out all mine iniquities.
Create in me a clean heart, O God; and renew a right spirit
within me. Cast me not away from thy presence;
and take not thy holy spirit from me.
Restore unto me the joy of thy salvation;
and uphold me with thy free spirit.
(Ps. 51:9–12)

Why He Wants Us to Become

WHY IS IT THAT THE Lord is so willing to save us, so anxious to bring us back to His presence and reward us with a true promised land? Why does He plead with us to allow Him to do this despite our repeated backsliding? The Lord gives us the answer through His prophet Jeremiah: "Yea, I have loved thee with an everlasting love: therefore with lovingkindness have I drawn thee" (Jer. 31:3). It is God's great, expansive, and everlasting love that causes Him to repeatedly reach out to us, to so consistently conciliate with us. Remember how Hosea compared God's love for us with the ardent love of a young groom, willing to take His beloved bride back at any time? "I will heal their backsliding, I will love them freely" (Hosea 14:4). As Elder Ned B. Roueché taught, having paid our ransom, the Savior loves each of us and reaches out to every one who will follow Him.[32]

But God's love doesn't merely inspire Him to take us back. God also sees what we can become. As President Dieter F. Uchtdorf taught, God is the Father of our spirits, and He sees each one of us as His child—as the person we are capable—and designed—to become as His child.[33] In other words, God's love for us, coupled with His vision of our potential, causes Him to make more of us than we had ever thought possible. As He promised the Israelites, "If ye hearken to these judgments, and keep, and do them, that the Lord thy God shall keep unto thee the covenant and the mercy which He sware unto thy fathers: And He will love thee, and bless thee, and multiply thee" (Deut. 7:12–13). What does it mean to be multiplied? A sense of that word for ancient Israel was certainly that they would become a numerous people. And in a way I think that aspect can apply for each of us in this life and the next. But I believe there are other ways God multiplies us. I think He exponentially increases the kernel of godliness within us all.

Being Born Again—A New Creature

Another phrase for this concept is being *born again*. We typically associate this concept with the New Testament or the Book of Mormon. However, it is also an important Old Testament theme.

Being *born again* is a notion we as Latter-day Saints often shy away from, mostly in reaction to what we perceive as erroneous beliefs of some of our Christian friends. I think we misunderstand both their beliefs and our own. The Book of Mormon is more emphatic about being born again than any other book of scripture. If anyone should understand and talk about being born again it should be us as Latter-day Saints. Alma seems as if he is speaking to us when he says, "And the Lord said unto me: Marvel not that all mankind, yea, men and women, all nations, kindreds, tongues and people, must be born again; yea, born of God, changed from their carnal and fallen state, to a state of righteousness, being redeemed of God, becoming His sons and daughters; and thus they become new creatures; and unless they do this, they can in nowise inherit the kingdom of God" (Mosiah 27:25–26).

We often talk about this as becoming a new creature in Christ, drawing on the language of Paul when he said, "therefore if any man be in Christ, He is a new creature" (2 Cor. 5:17). But what does it mean to be born again or become a new creature in Christ? While a full treatment of this essential and exhilarating topic would be too lengthy for this chapter, we will cover the essential aspects here so that we may fully appreciate what we can hope for as a result of God's love for us.

I believe that being born again means that the power of the Atonement enters your being through the Holy Ghost and changes your nature into something more godly. It means that by the grace of God the person you were before is gone, and some aspect of your character or nature becomes more heavenly. Soon after that experience the strongest effect of it will begin to disperse. But I believe that once we have had the experience we are permanently changed. These experiences are what cause us to try again. For most of us, it doesn't happen just once; we must be born again, and again, and again. Often the change that comes results from the Lord identifying a part of our fallen nature that really needs help, providing experiences for us that will help us focus on that flaw, force us to turn to Him, and reshape us in a more godly way through the atoning power of Christ when we really do seek His help.

The Lord illustrates this concept very well for Jeremiah. He told Jeremiah to go watch a potter who was making a vessel out of clay. As the potter spun, formed, and molded the vessel on his wheel, some kind of flaw occurred. The vessel was forming the wrong way. So the potter took the half-formed mass of clay, pressed it back into a lump, and started over. Now he formed a new vessel—this time one without a flaw (see Jer. 18:1–6).

What a wonderful metaphor for being born again. In order to correct our flaws, the Lord will make us into something new. It may not always be fun, but in the end we will become something better than we were before. Jeremiah spoke of how the Lord would do this for Israel—His wicked and fallen people who were on the verge of destruction because of what they had become: "At the same time, saith the Lord, will I be the God of all the families of Israel, and they shall be my people. Thus saith the Lord, The people *which were* left of the sword found grace in the wilderness; *even* Israel, when I went to cause Him to rest" (Jer. 31:1–2). Stated in more modern terminology, those who survived the attack of Babylon and were carried away would find grace, would again become God's people, and would find rest. In other words, God would help them become a new covenant people, just as He will help you and me become a new person within the covenant. After the pain of Him working with us, we will be born again; we will become better than we were before. What great hope there is in this message! We need not give up when we confront ourselves with the things that are wrong about us. Instead we can realize that the Lord is willing to help us through and to bring us out the other side a better person—no matter how long it takes.

C. S. Lewis described the process so aptly: "Christ says, 'Give me All. I don't want so much of your time and so much of your money and so much of your work: I want You. I have not come to torment your natural self, but to kill it. No half-measures are any good. I don't want to cut off a branch here and a branch there, I want to have the whole tree down. I don't want to drill the tooth, or crown it, or stop it, but to have it out. Hand over the whole natural self, all the desires which you think innocent as well as the ones you think wicked—the whole outfit. I will give you a new self instead. In fact, I will give you Myself: My own will shall become yours.'"[34]

This same concept is described in a different way in the Old Testament. For example, Moses taught Israel that "the Lord thy God will circumcise thine heart, and the heart of thy seed, to love the Lord thy God with all thine heart and with all thy soul, that thou mayest live" (Deut. 30:6).

Moses was not alone in describing how the Lord could change our hearts. Ezekiel was even more clear. Consider the group Ezekiel was talking to. In his day, Israel had been incredibly wicked, repeatedly ignoring the Lord's requests and warnings. Few of us could possibly have done as many wrong things as had Israel. Yet even if we have, hear what the Lord promises Israel: "Therefore say, Thus saith the Lord God; I will even gather you from the people, and assemble you out of the countries where ye have been scattered, and I will give you the land of Israel. And they shall come thither, and they shall take away all the detestable things thereof and all the abominations thereof from thence. And I will give them one heart, and I will put a new spirit within you; and I will take the stony heart out of their flesh, and will give them an heart of flesh" (Ezek. 11:17–19).

What a wonderful promise! Wherever we are spiritually, God is trying to gather us in to Him if we will just put our sinful things away. We will be given a new heart! There is nothing more we can ask for. If we want to be exalted, we have to understand that exalted beings have a different nature, a different heart. Through the power of the Atonement we can have our natures changed, our hearts remade. And to heighten its wonder, this is a promise extended to a wicked people—a people who had rejected the word of God and were in the midst of experiencing vast punishment. If God extends such hope to them, how much more must He extend to each of us in our own lives? The Lord's message, delivered through Ezekiel, is one of hope and promise.

Elder David A. Bednar described this process in general conference he taught that the essence of the gospel brings about a change in our very nature as we rely on "the merits, and mercy, and grace of the Holy Messiah" (2 Ne. 2:8). Our choice to follow the Savior, then, is a choice to be changed and reborn.[35]

The change is described so clearly in the story of Saul. When Samuel anointed Saul as king, he told the newly anointed ruler what would happen when he left Samuel's place and met a group of prophets: "And the Spirit of the Lord will come upon thee, and thou shalt prophesy with them, and shalt be turned into another man" (1 Sam. 10:6). When Saul left Samuel, we are told, "God gave Him another heart" (1 Sam. 10:9). What marvelous descriptions! To be turned into another man, to be given another heart! Isn't this exactly what we yearn for when we confront ourselves and our own unworthiness? In those moments when we see the starkness of our failures to live up to the godliness we know is within us, don't we more than anything want to have another heart and become another person? From the story of Saul we learn how available that is—that God really will do it for us. Saul became another man, and so can we.

Even more comforting is the fact that this was not the end of the story for Saul. After this mighty change that was wrought in His heart, He did well. But Saul kept messing up, sometimes in extremely serious ways. I find it so comforting to know that God did not give up on Saul; even when Saul messed up again, God continued to work with him. Despite Saul's many mistakes and sins, even in some of His worst moments, the Spirit of the Lord overcame him and he began to prophesy again (see 1 Sam. 19). Sadly, Saul did not seem to ever fully come around. But the message of hope for us is that we can see in Saul's story the kind of change the Lord can work on us and how the

Lord will give us more chances. He will help us to be born again, and again, and again, offering innumerable chances as long as we keep trying to come back to Him.

As mentioned earlier, the comforting thing is that as we are given second, third, and seven times seventy chances, the Lord will provide transforming and overwhelming help to us in becoming something new and greater than we were. Steven Covey explained this cogently as He spoke about our need for second chances:

> We can't fully overcome these habits and impacted tendencies by ourselves. Our own resolves, our own will, our own effort—all this is necessary but is not sufficient. We need the transforming power of the Savior, born of faith in Him and His atoning sacrifice and of entering into a contract with him. In such a contract, made in ordinance work and in private prayer, we covenant, or promise, or witness to take upon ourselves His name and to keep His commandments. He, in turn, promises us to give us His spirit, which, if we are true to our promises, will renew and strengthen and transform us. In this way we combine our power with the power of the Almighty.[36]

It is only when we underestimate the importance of covenants, the magnitude of God's love and patience, and the power of Christ's Atonement that we doubt what He can make of us. When we realize God loves us enough to never give up on us, when we remember that His covenant ties us to Him and gives us access to the sanctifying power of the Atonement, and when we recognize the overwhelming power of the Atonement, then we can rest assured that as long as we are willing to keep trying the Lord is able to make us into new creatures. Eventually He will even make us into Christlike creatures.

The Parable of the Unfinished Painting

It is crucial that we realize and remember the new creature God will help us become. We must stay cognizant of God's loving desire *and* ability to make us into something greater than we can conceive.

This need is conveyed well by what a friend of mine calls "the parable of the unfinished painting." A painter and presenter of some renown, Lynde Mott often talks about the process of creating a painting. In her mind she can envision what it will look like when it is finished. But as she begins to apply layers of color to a canvas, it never looks good to her; whenever she takes a step back and looks at what she has done she is dismayed. The painting always looks terrible in her eyes. She is tempted to throw it away because it looks so bad. But because she knows the process, understands the vision, and is sure she can work the paint into that vision, she is able to reassure herself that she can indeed make it look good. She knows that when the process is through, everything will come together to create something attractive. She perseveres, stroke by stroke, and when she is done she is finally able to behold something striking and beautiful.

To create a painting, Lynde paints in layers. As friends or family members watch, they often see her put some color or layer on and think to themselves, *Oh no, you just ruined it!* But Lynde has seen the end product in her mind and knows how to create. Once all of the strokes and swirls coalesce into a comprehensive whole, the painting is beautiful.

So it is with our lives—we constantly look at ourselves as we progress. It's easy to forget that we are just that—a work in progress. We shouldn't be surprised that the partially finished product appears to have flaws. When Lynde paints, she often paints with colors that seem too light; someone looking at the painting would see it similar to an overexposed photograph. But Lynde knows the kind of glaze she will apply at the end and the effect it will have on the tones in the painting. The painting will actually look wrong for all but the last five minutes of the one hundred hours it takes to create it. It is only in the last five minutes that it all comes together and takes on the look she has envisioned all along—a look of stunning beauty. What a loss it would have been if the painting had been discarded partway through the process! This is all the more true for you and me.

We have to remember that the great artist who is creating something more of us *will* finish His painting if we allow Him to. He will make us into something more grand and beautiful than we have ever imagined. As He works with our flawed and imperfect material, as He carefully shapes and changes us, we may not always like what we see. This is because we haven't seen the end product, *but He has*. Stroke by stroke, line by line, layer by layer, the Lord creates. We may not understand how some experiences or struggles could possibly improve us. We have to trust that the flaws we see are really part of the painting process and that if we turn ourselves over to our loving Father, He will make us into a masterpiece. Through the atoning power of His Son, God will make us into Christlike creatures. We will become beings of glory. "Eye hath not seen, nor ear heard, neither have entered into the heart of man, the things which God hath prepared for them that love him" (1 Cor. 2:9).

We are incapable of understanding the divine potential within us, of envisioning the kind of being we really are and will become. Instead we must have faith in God's perspective, just as Samuel did when he anointed David to be king of Israel. After Samuel anointed the tallest man in Israel as king, the Lord sent him to anoint another. When Samuel arrived at Jesse's home in Bethlehem, as he had been directed, he saw a number of men who seemed kingly in stature. To everyone's surprise, the Lord selected the youngest—a ruddy boy named David. None of them could see it, though he was beautiful for a youth. Despite his youth and a lack of any signs of what he would become, the Lord looked at David and saw the king. While Jesse and even the prophet Samuel saw a young shepherd, God saw the greatest king Israel would ever have. And so God sees in us the kings and queens that we are unable to recognize in ourselves. Our faulty vision does not change the accuracy of God's knowledge of who we really are. The Lord's view of our true, glorious nature and future is, in fact, reality.

Sometimes it is difficult to really believe these things because we can remember the things we have done wrong. In our weak moments, our fallen nature and Satan himself remind us of our failings. Where God sees our struggles as another layer of paint in an unfinished masterpiece, Satan would have us focus on the partial picture and view it as a flaw. He preys on the fact that all of us regret certain actions; He capitalizes on opportunities to remind us we have done wrong, glossing over the fact that some bumps are really texture that will add to the picture the master is making. A few verses from Ezekiel give us enough ammunition to send Satan packing. Ezekiel taught that if we were willing to try again, God would forgive, forget, and bring us back to Him. In other words, the portions of our perfecting process that don't look good will be covered brush stroke by brush stroke—strokes that will bring us closer to completion. In Hebrew the word that we translate as "atonement" is *kippur*, which literally means "to cover." It is this covering aspect of the Atonement that Ezekiel draws on.

This imagery is found throughout Ezekiel, and while it is sometimes discussed on the level of Israel as a whole, it is depicted in such a way as to leave no doubt that the Lord is talking about each Israelite individual. The Lord assured His people of the chance to repent, regardless of what they had done wrong, when He taught them, "If the wicked will **turn** from all His sins that He hath committed, and keep all my statutes, and do that which is lawful and right, He shall surely live, He shall not die. All His transgressions that He hath committed, they shall not be mentioned unto him: in His righteousness that He hath done He shall live" (Ezek. 18:21–22; emphasis added).

As a point of emphasis, the Lord almost immediately repeated that promise, making it emphatic: "When the wicked man **turneth** away from His wickedness that He hath committed, and doeth that which is lawful and right, He shall save His soul alive. Because He considereth, and **turneth** away from all His transgressions that He hath committed, He shall surely live, He shall not die" (Ezek. 18:27–28; emphasis added). The concept is so important it receives yet another iteration later in Ezekiel: "I say unto the wicked, Thou shalt surely die; if He **turn** from His sin, and do that which is lawful and right; if the wicked restore the pledge, give again that He had robbed, walk in the statutes of life, without committing iniquity; He shall surely live, He shall not die. None of His sins that He hath committed shall be mentioned unto him: He hath done that which is lawful and right; He shall surely live" (Ezek. 33:14–16; emphasis added).

Think of this wonderful promise. While I feel I have led a pretty good life, there are certainly things I wish I had never done, things that would make me cringe and want to hide if they were brought up among my friends, colleagues, or ward members. These are not terrible things, but I wish I had never done them. Yet the Lord has made it clear what is available if I repent, if I turn away and endeavor to right those wrongs.

I find great comfort from the promise that all my transgressions "shall not be mentioned" to me again. They will be covered over, and instead I will find life. An immense amount of relief, peace, and comfort can flow through all of us due to this promise. Surely we have all done things we shouldn't have, things that have separated us from God in some measure and things we regret. But God promises that as we turn to Him, it is as if these things had not been, for they will not be mentioned.

This wonderful assurance is followed by a heartfelt plea: "Cast away from you all your transgressions, whereby ye have transgressed; and make you a new heart and a new spirit: for why will ye die, O house of Israel? For I have no pleasure in the death of Him that dieth, saith the Lord God: wherefore **turn** yourselves, and live ye" (Ezek. 18:31–32; emphasis added). We have read this verse before, but think of it in the context of God promising us that if we turn to Him again He will not mention our wickedness. Can't you sense the Lord's love and desire in this plea? Can't you feel Him begging us to turn from our transgressions so that we can receive a new heart? Clearly He would much rather accept this than that we die in our sins and be punished. The knowledge that repentance means our sins are mentioned no more adds power to His last appeal: "Turn, and live." In the end, it is as simple as that. We need not worry about the things we have already done. Instead we just need to turn from our worldly desire, from our affinity for sin, from those things that distract us from God. All we need is to turn, return to Him, and then, through the grace and power of the Atonement, we will live.

Better—Stronger Than Before

Not only will we live, but we will be new creatures. We will become beings of a higher order through the power of our loving God. When we struggle with our sins and shortcomings and turn to God, through His grace and power we will be better than we were before. Zechariah also teaches this when the Lord speaks through Him to talk about Israel's future. After their great destruction at the hands of Babylon, Israel returned to God. When they did so, He delivered them again. While Zechariah taught during this period, He knew that Israel would fall away from God again and experience even greater destruction. Zechariah's promise was that even after all this, God would make Israel into something greater than they had been before. As you read Zechariah's teachings, remember that what the Lord says to and of Israel He says to and of you and me as Israelites.

After all the wickedness of Israel and their ensuing destruction, Jerusalem and Israel were not just to be reestablished, they were to be made greater than they had ever been. Jerusalem would exceed her walls, spreading forth in great growth. As if this were not enough, Zechariah assures us that the Lord Himself would be with Jerusalem: "Sing and rejoice, O daughter of Zion: for, lo, I come, and I will dwell in the midst of thee, saith the Lord" (Zech. 2:10).

What a wonderful promise! My choices and actions may have brought me to despair. I may be looking around at the ashes and rubble of my life. Perhaps it is not even that dramatic. Perhaps I just feel that my spirituality, my capability, my desirability, or my potential has been reduced to debris and burning embers. Despite how silly, stupid, or maybe even downright wicked I have been, if I will once again turn to the Lord, He will make of me more than I have ever been. I will become a greater, more capable, more spiritually beautiful person than I had thought possible. And as this change occurs, the Lord himself will dwell with me. He promises us a companionship that we all yearn for. Satan would have us believe that our sins have precluded us from His presence, but the Lord tells us that even after sin and affliction He will increase us and bless us with His sweet presence. Satan is wrong, and we must not believe him. We can "rejoice," for God will dwell with us. He will build us up in a way that is beyond our imagination.

The first three chapters of Zechariah really seem to be all about the idea of God making us greater than we could conceive—despite what we have been in the past. Remember that in Zechariah's vision of Joshua the priest, a mitre awaited Joshua after he was cleansed from his filth. He was not just restored to being a pure priest but was made a priest and a king in the vision. His last state was higher than his first.

Zechariah frequently teaches the concept of being made greater than we have ever been. In Chapter 8, the Lord speaks to Israel of their eventual return to Him, contrasting it with their earlier days:

For before these days there was no hire for man, nor any hire for beast; neither was there any peace to Him that went out or came in because of the affliction: for I set all men every one against His neighbour.

But now I will not be unto the residue of this people as in the former days, saith the Lord of hosts.

For the seed shall be prosperous; the vine shall give her fruit, and the ground shall give her increase, and the heavens shall give their dew; and I will cause the remnant of this people to possess all these things.

And it shall come to pass, that as ye were a curse among the heathen, O house of Judah, and house of Israel; so will I save you, and ye shall be a blessing: fear not, but let your hands be strong.

For thus saith the Lord of hosts; As I thought to punish you, when your fathers provoked me to wrath, saith the Lord of hosts, and I repented not:

So again have I thought in these days to do well unto Jerusalem and to the house of Judah: fear ye not. (Zech. 8:10–15)

After all that they had done, and after all of the punishments they had received, Israel would prosper like never before. They would become a blessing to the earth. And so it is with each of us. As Isaiah said, "A little one shall become a thousand, and a small one a strong nation" (Isa. 60:22). Elsewhere, when the Lord speaks of an Israel that He had scattered and then brought back—using imagery reminiscent of the idea of "covering" or "atoning" our sins— Jehovah said, "Remember these, O Jacob and Israel; for thou are my servant: I have formed thee; thou art my servant: O Israel, thou shalt not be forgotten of me. I have blotted out, as a thick cloud, thy transgressions, and, as a cloud, thy sins: **return** unto me; for I have redeemed thee" (Isa. 44:21–22; emphasis added).

Later Isaiah spoke of how, after Israel's punishment had brought them low and made them ugly, the Lord would beautify them, making Israel an "eternal excellency, a joy of many generations" and promising that "the sun shall be no more thy light by day; neither for brightness shall the moon give light unto thee: but the Lord shall be unto thee an everlasting light, and thy God thy glory" (Isa. 60:15, 19).

Remember how, after responding well to chastisement, Job was doubly blessed? This is exactly what the Lord is trying to do. If we work with Him in His way, He will make us twice as much—no, exponentially more—than we were before He began His process of covenantal care.

A paramount example of this is Joseph who was sold into Egypt. Note how many of the themes we have talked about are part of his experience. Joseph was loved by his Father. Even in his youth, when he may not have seemed like much, it was clear that God saw Joseph as the great ruler he would become. From early in Joseph's youth God hinted at what He already saw in the boy by giving him prophetic dreams that symbolized his future.

Though Joseph was abandoned and betrayed by his brothers, he stayed faithful to the Lord. Going from Potiphar's chief steward to prison must have seemed like backsliding indeed. Joseph could have seen his arrest and imprisonment at the hands of Potiphar as a punishment that came because of his obedience. Instead, he remained full of faith, determined to serve the Lord. Because the Lord had covenanted with Israel that He would save His family, and because Joseph was part of that covenant, God kept working with Joseph, aiming at delivering Joseph himself and then helping Joseph deliver the rest of Israel.

The chance for the butler to tell Pharaoh about Joseph probably seemed like Joseph's last, great hope. Even after the butler forgot Joseph, it was not too late. When this hope seemed to have passed him by he did not give up his faith in the Lord. He continued his struggle in prison (probably a mining camp or something similar) and showed his willingness to serve the Lord faithfully in whatever circumstances he found himself. Joseph demonstrated his belief in the power of God while the Lord—stroke by stroke, layer by layer—made Joseph into the kind of person he needed to be. I do not profess to know in what ways Joseph needed to improve, but I am convinced that Joseph's difficulties in life helped to refine him, and that the hand of a loving God was involved in such a way that Joseph became what God needed him to become. God was with him, gently—and sometimes not so gently—bringing Joseph back to Him. In the process, He helped Joseph bring others to Him.

Eventually Joseph was raised to a position that was greater and higher than anything he had ever imagined. Pharaoh took him from prison, discarded his prison raiment, and put upon him vestures of fine linen and the signs of a ruler. In receiving a ring and a gold chain, Joseph was given the Egyptian equivalent of a fair mitre upon his head. He then found himself able to do good for countless people and to help his family more than he would have ever considered while a youth. The Lord obviously knew from the beginning. When looking at Joseph in his father's fields, God looked at a shepherd boy but saw the great savior and ruler of Egypt. Through a circuitous and arduous path, He made Joseph greater than Joseph would ever have asked for himself.

In my own life I have found that when things don't work out the way I thought they would, it was usually because God had something better in mind. Often His plans required that I readjust my expectations and thinking, but I find there is always more in store for me than I had planned for myself.

President Ezra Taft Benson spoke of this when he taught, "Men and women who turn their lives over to God will find out that He can make a lot more out of their lives than they can."[37] If my understanding of the images and teachings of the Old Testament and other scriptures is correct, we will become something greater than we can possibly understand right now through the gift and power of God. Our task is to keep coming unto Him. No matter how often we falter along the way, no matter how filthy we become on the journey, we must press on. God has both the desire and ability to change us. We just have to keep coming.

CHAPTER EIGHT
COMING BACK

*Thou in thy mercy hast led forth the people which thou hast redeemed:
thou hast guided them in thy strength unto thy holy habitation.*
(Ex. 15:13)

*Purge me with hyssop, and I shall be clean: wash me, and I shall be
whiter than snow. Make me to hear joy and gladness; that the bones
which thou hast broken may rejoice.*
(Ps. 51:7–8)

The Path of Love

When Latter-day Saints talk about the path back to God, we
usually speak of a strait and narrow way and usually refer to the
gate of baptism. This is doctrinally true, profoundly significant, and
cannot be overemphasized. We understand these elements of the path
and know we must conform in order to return to God. But I'd like
to speak of other aspects of the way back to God, exploring some
principles that undergird the entrance through the gate and that
enable us to endure to the end once we have mounted the path.

Since all commandments are based on principles, I think we can
turn to the greatest of commandments to find the greatest of guiding
principles. As we know, a lawyer asked the Savior which was the
greatest commandment in the law (see Matt. 22:36). In answer, the
Savior quoted from the law as found in the Old Testament, repeating
for the lawyer part of what is probably the most significant verse for
all of Judaism, then and now:

> Hear, O Israel: The Lord our God *is* one Lord:
> And thou shalt love the Lord thy God with all thine heart, and with all thy soul, and with all thy might.
> And these words, which I command thee this day, shall be in thine heart:
> And thou shalt teach them diligently unto thy children, and shalt talk of them when thou sittest in thine house, and when thou walkest by the way, and when thou liest down, and when thou risest up.
> And thou shalt bind them for a sign upon thine hand, and they shall be as frontlets between thine eyes.
> And thou shalt write them upon the posts of thy house, and on thy gates. (Deut. 6:4–9)

The Lord's instructions make it clear how much He wished to emphasize the principle. It was so important for every Israelite to learn to love the Lord that Israelite families were to teach it, talk about it, write it and put it where they would be constantly reminded of it. Everything is based on the love of God. This is the great commandment because it naturally leads to all others. It especially leads to the second great commandment, which is to love others.

The relationship between loving God and loving others is made clear in a few places. The Lord instructed Israel to love others because He had loved them (see Deut. 10:18–19). The Savior implied the relationship between those when He spoke with the lawyer, saying that the second commandment was like unto the first (see Matt. 22:39). Many have spoken of the implicit relationship in the Ten Commandments since the first several seem to focus on our relationship with God and the others on our relationship with our fellow man.

The same can be said of the beatitudes, especially as recorded in 3 Nephi. Another part of that sermon is explicit about how our relationship with God is intertwined with our relationship with our fellow man. The Lord said, "Therefore, if ye shall come unto me, or shall desire to come unto me, and rememberest that thy brother hath aught against thee—Go thy way unto thy brother, and first be reconciled to thy brother, and then come unto me with full purpose of heart, and I will receive you" (3 Ne. 12:23–24).

Clearly we cannot come to the Lord if we are not treating our fellow man correctly. In many ways this is reflected in the famous story about Joseph Smith's failure to translate from the Book of Mormon immediately after having had some kind of disagreement with Emma. Soon after he went out to ask the Lord why he couldn't translate, he returned home and asked Emma's forgiveness with real intent. He was then able to translate. Like Joseph, if we really need to receive direction from God and we are serious about trying to approach Him, we too must make things right with our fellow man. We must "first be reconciled with [our] brother," and then we can come unto the Lord. The way we feel about God's children affects our relationship with our divine parent.

I also believe the more we love God the more we will naturally love His other children. When we love God with all our hearts we will more easily and more deeply love those whom He loves. As the Prophet Joseph Smith said, "The nearer we get to our Heavenly Father, the more we are disposed to look with compassion on perishing souls; we feel that we want to take them upon our shoulders, and cast their sins behind our backs."[38]

It all starts with that first, great commandment, outlined so eloquently in Deuteronomy. The language indicates how emphatic God is about how much we must love Him. He does not just say we must love God, nor even that we must love Him with all our heart. We must love Him with all our heart, with all our soul, and with all our might (see Deut. 6:4–5; Deut. 10:12). Moses, who received the command from God, was so emphatic that he repeated it in Deuteronomy 6:4–5; 7:9; 10:12; 11:1; 11:22; 13:3; 19:9; 30:16; and 30:20. Joshua, who was with Moses, also reminded the next generation of Israelites of that specific command (see Josh. 22:5, 23:11).

Israel was instructed to post the Deuteronomy 6 verses about loving God in various places so they could keep it ever before them. Today we must find our own way to keep the need to love God continually before our spiritual eyes. God also commanded them to teach it to their children. Do we find ways to continually teach the paramount importance of this commandment in our families?

Although it is crucial that we never lose focus on loving God, once we really have learned to concentrate on this commandment, we can move to others. The more we love God, the more we love others. The more we love others, the more we are able to love God. This is a pattern that will help us spiral toward heaven.

There is another reason why it is so important to love God: Such love helps us to do everything for the right reason. Because blessings are predicated upon obedience, it is possible to be motivated to obey commandments just so that we can receive the promised blessings. While that kind of obedience can help us become better, it has a limited capacity to do so. It is obedience out of selfishness. It is far better to obey because we love God and want to please Him. For example, we can pay tithing because we want to have the devourer rebuked and the windows of heaven opened for us (see Mal. 3:10–11). But it is better to pay tithing because we love God and want both to please Him and to do all we can to further His cause. This will evoke a far greater change in us. It will go much further toward our becoming more Christlike.

The Savior's primary motives were love for others and, above all, love for His Father. If we truly want to become more like the Savior, these should be our motives as well. The more we love God, the more we will do the right thing *because* we love Him. The more we obey out of love, the more Christlike we become and the happier we will be. Obeying and helping others for the right reason—out of love—is an essential part of the pattern that will help us spiral toward God. In the Old Testament God repeatedly asked Israel to do the things He had commanded them to do for the right reason, typically focusing on the need to love. Micah explained that God would not be as pleased with thousands of offerings or rivers of anointing oil as He would with Israel extending mercy and love to both man and God (see Micah 6:6–8). Clearly the Lord is concerned with our motives for obedience, and He wants those motives to be based on love of God and man.

I think there is a key element we often overlook in this pattern that would lead us to more fully love God. John the Beloved explained it in his masterful discourse on love: "We love him, because He first loved us" (1 John 4:19). David says the same thing another way, highlighting one of the ways we can feel God's love: "I love the Lord, because He hath heard my voice and my supplications" (Ps. 116:1). The idea that we love God because He loves us is deeply profound. Our love for God is inspired by His love for us. The more we feel His love for us, the more we will love Him. The more we love Him, the more we will be propelled forward in the spiraling path to be with Him again. It all starts with God's love for us.

However, if we don't feel God's love for us, our love for Him—and thus for others—will not deepen and progress as it should. I believe it is impossible to move forward on this path if we do not deeply feel God's love, if we are not convicted and transfixed by that overwhelming and penetrating power. God loves us, but we must allow ourselves to feel that love.

We must not fall into the trap of thinking that we need to earn God's love. God plainly taught ancient Israel that He did not love them because of their greatness, but because of His love and His covenant (see Deut. 7:7–8). He was simultaneously clear that His ability to act on that love and deliver His people was connected with their love of Him (see Deut. 7:9).

One of the most famous symbols in all of Mormondom was explained by the angel to Nephi as he saw the same vision his father had beheld: "And the angel said unto me: Behold the Lamb of God, yea, even the Son of the Eternal Father! Knowest thou the meaning of the tree which thy father saw? And I answered him, saying: Yea, it is the love of God, which sheddeth itself abroad in the hearts of the children of men; wherefore, it is the most desirable above all things. And He spake unto me, saying: Yea, and the most joyous to the soul" (1 Ne. 11:21–23).

The wonderful and maddening thing about this scripture is its ambiguity. Here we are presented with something more desirable and more joyous than anything. This is clearly something we would want. Yet the grammar of the phrase *love of God* makes it impossible to determine whether it refers to our love of God or God's love of us. It can be taken either way.

Many times I have pondered which is meant. I have studied the context of the surrounding verses and the way in which either concept works in other places in the scriptures. I have searched teachings by prophets about this verse. While I in no way imply that I have the ability to declare what the phrase means, I believe that both interpretations apply. However, it seems that it leans slightly toward God's love for us.

One of the reasons I say this is because the angel, in the way he asks the question, implies that the interpretation of the fruit is tied up with the Lamb of God (drawing on Old Testament Passover imagery). The Lamb of God is the most powerful and visible expression of God's love for us: "God so loved the world, that He gave His only begotten Son" (John 3:16). If Christ is tied to the meaning of the fruit of the tree, and if Christ is the manifestation of God's love for us, then the fruit must in some way represent God's love for us. This interpretation is strengthened by the fact that after explaining the symbolism of the fruit, Nephi's vision moved on to the Savior's ministry and His blessing of people's lives.

Yet how is it that only some people come to partake of the fruit of the tree? Doesn't God love all of us? Of course He does, but not all people allow themselves to feel that love. It "sheddeth itself abroad in the hearts of the children of men," but not all men do what is necessary to open their hearts to it. However, at least in my own life, no experience is so sweet and desirable as the times that I am suffused in God's love. It changes everything. When I feel how much God loves me, I feel more desire for righteousness, more love for others, and more hope. When we feel how much God loves us, we also catch a glimpse of how much He loves others, which helps us to love them more. When we feel how much He loves us it causes us to reevaluate our own worth. We know what potential lies within us. We can realize what God will do for us, if we will only let Him. Paul taught that we had access to the Savior's grace through hope, which we could have "because the love of God is shed abroad in our hearts by the Holy Ghost which is given unto us. For when we were yet without strength, in due time Christ died for the ungodly . . . but God commendeth His love toward us, in that, while we were yet sinners, Christ died for us" (Rom. 5:1–8).

The question is, how do we come to feel God's love more deeply? The answer seems to be that we must allow the Spirit to teach us of this love, to impart the love to us, and to carry it deep into our souls. The key is to do those things that will invite the Spirit to convey God's love into our hearts. As Moses taught Israel, the ability to love

God was a gift that came as God changes our hearts (see Deut. 30:6). We must avail ourselves of every opportunity to feel the Spirit and to learn of God's love, then that love will seep deeply into our souls and settle into our very fabric. Part of this process includes searching the scriptures in a manner that will allow the Spirit to teach us what they mean. One of the things they teach most abundantly, if we will only look for it, is how much God loves us.

A focus on ourselves will restrict us from these opportunities. We will not be able to forgive others, to serve them, or to love them if we are focusing on ourselves. We will not be able to love God as we should if we love ourselves too much or love ourselves more than we love God. We will not be able to feel God's love for us if we are concentrating on what others think of us. As we forget ourselves, we will be more able to feel God's love.

There are a thousand things we can do to feel God's love. In reality, most of the sermons you and I have ever heard or read concentrate on various things that will further enable us to feel of God's love. The gospel is about Christ and His Atonement, the ultimate expression of that love. Thus, everything in the gospel points us toward this love. As we know, there are also a thousand obstacles to really living the gospel. There are so many things that could get in our way. Perhaps the biggest obstacle is our own fallen nature. As we combine this nature with any number of other things, we impede our own progress toward God. Giving up this nature allows us to feel the circle of His love and thus speeds us toward Him.

Overcoming through God

Here is an absolute truth: In our efforts to return to God, there are no obstacles too large. This would not be true if we were on this journey alone. But we are not. We have God by our side, and with the aid of God nothing can prevent us from completing the journey and becoming what He wants us to become. Surely "The Lord is my shepherd; I shall not want. He maketh me to lie down in green pastures: He leadeth me beside the still waters. He restoreth my soul: He leadeth me in the paths of righteousness for His name's sake. Yea, though I walk through the valley of the shadow of death, I will fear no evil: for thou art with me . . . Surely goodness and mercy shall follow me all the days of my life" (Ps. 23:1–6). What a comfort to have God as our guide and protector on this journey. It is the only way to ensure success in our attempt to be with God again. If we really make God our shepherd then success is guaranteed.

God wants us to return to Him, to come into and inherit the true promised land. In fact, He would like for us to inherit all that He has. Our own nature, death, and hell are the greatest obstacles in our way. However, none of these obstacles is problematic with God on our side. As Isaiah told ancient Israel, "He giveth power to the faint; and to them that have no might He increaseth strength. Even the youths shall faint and be weary, and the young men shall utterly fall: But they that wait upon the LORD shall renew their strength; they shall mount up with wings as eagles; they shall run, and not be weary; and they shall walk, and not faint" (Isa. 40:29–31).

As you read this verse, think of Joshua and the children of Israel. They encountered their first large army, representing several of the biggest cities of Canaan, just outside of Gibeon, about five miles north of Jerusalem. The Lord not only helped them to be victorious in battle by amplifying their own abilities, but He assisted them with huge hailstones. As their enemies fled, hoping to run until the cover of darkness hid them, the Lord held the moon and sun still, allowing Israel to slay their enemies. In this case Israel had marched all night to be in the right place at the right time. They had certainly put forth their best effort and literally put their lives on the line. But they were not enough on their own. So, the Lord helped them by sending hailstones and by extending the day. He must have also helped them to not become weary or faint. Not only had they made a several-thousand-foot climb during their all-night journey, but they fought throughout the day and into what would have been the next night, chasing their enemies across great distances and over hilly and difficult terrain (see Josh. 10). It seems as if these unwearying Israelites were born up by eagles' wings, finding success through the Lord that was beyond the reach of their own natural strength. So it can be with us.

While undoubtedly there is much *we* need to do in order to return to God, we often overemphasize this in our own lives. Please do not misunderstand me: We have to give it everything we have.

There is a great effort required on our part. We know that we are saved by grace only after *all* we can do (see 2 Ne. 25:23). But I often witness a tendency to focus on the "all we can do" part and not the "grace" part. In my experience Latter-day Saints spend their time talking and thinking about the things they must do and the things they have failed to do, but give little thought to the fact that whatever we do or don't do will never be enough without the Savior's grace. Such a misplaced emphasis will always lead to frustration, failure, and eventual hopelessness, because we cannot make it by relying on our own strength, no matter how strong we are. Doing so is essentially trusting in the arm of flesh—a course that will never work. If we want to receive salvation and experience joy, peace, and hope along the way, then we must feel to say that which the psalmist did: "Some trust in chariots, and some in horses: but we will remember the name of the Lord our God" (Ps. 20:7).

Think of what our loving Lord teaches us again and again through the symbolism of real events in the Old Testament. As He time after time brought the Israelites into the promised land and helped them inherit it, the Lord helped little Israel overcome the obstacles of the Egyptians, Amorites, Hivites, Hittites, Perizzites, Jebusites, Canaanites, Amonites, Moabites, Midianites, Gergashites, Gibeonites, Edomites, Philistines, Assyrians, and Babylonians. We all know that overcoming each of these was a miracle wrought by the hand of God. If this was what the Lord did, again and again, to bring Israel into the promised land, what can't He do to bring you back to Him in the true promised land? Surely God can bring us home—including you.

And oh, how He wants to! He wants nothing more than to bring us back to Him as the kind of creatures we both want us to be. Some of the most touching language in the scriptures comes when God expresses how much He would like to bring us back. Listen to the Lord describe His efforts to the Nephites:

> O ye people of these great cities which have fallen, who are descendants of Jacob, yea, who are of the house of Israel, how oft have I gathered you as a hen gathereth her chickens under her wings, and have nourished you.

> And again, how oft would I have gathered you as a hen
> gathereth her chickens under her wings, yea, O ye people
> of the house of Israel, who have fallen; yea, O ye people
> of the house of Israel, ye that dwell at Jerusalem, as ye that
> have fallen; yea, how oft would I have gathered you as a hen
> gathereth her chickens, and ye would not.
>
> O ye house of Israel whom I have spared, how oft will I
> gather you as a hen gathereth her chickens under her wings,
> if ye will repent and **return** unto me with full purpose of
> heart. (3 Ne. 10:4–6; emphasis added)

Did you notice the tenses the Savior used as He talked about gathering and protecting His children? With the loving image of a mother protecting and comforting her children with her own body, He says He *would have* gathered them, He *has* gathered them, and He *will* gather His children. There is no point in time when the Lord has not been trying to gather, guide, and protect His children.

Speaking to these same Nephites of the transgressors among them, the Lord said, "ye shall not cast him out of your synagogues, or your places of worship, for unto such shall ye continue to minister; for ye know not but what they will **return** and repent, and come unto me with full purpose of heart, and I shall heal them" (3 Ne. 18:32; emphasis added). What a comforting image: The Lord does not want any of us to be cast out because He hopes that we will eventually return to Him, in which case He stands ready to heal us. I am so grateful for the constant opportunity to be healed.

Sister Anne C. Pingree echoed these feelings when she taught that the image of the Savior rising "with healing in his wings" (3 Ne. 25:2) applies to each one of us—and that He will gather us and bless us if we will choose to come unto Him.[39] Healing and guidance are the things the Lord offers us, the very things we—the spiritually wounded, sick, and weary—need on our way.

The Gift of Joy

The Lord's love caused Him to teach us of the plan, to enact the plan, and to continue to try to help us succeed in the plan. The same loving kindness, longsuffering, and mercy that caused Him to suffer for our sins also moves Him to unfailingly, unceasingly, and unwearyingly reach out to us. Joseph F. Smith said, "Jesus had not finished his work when his body was slain, neither did he finish it after his resurrection from the dead; although he had accomplished the purpose for which he then came to the earth, he had not fulfilled all his work. And when will he? Not until he has redeemed and saved every son and daughter of our father Adam that have been or ever will be born upon this earth to the end of time, except the sons of perdition. That is his mission."[40]

We can rest assured of the Lord's power to accomplish His mission if we will only let Him: "The Lord thy God in the midst of thee is mighty; he will save, he will rejoice over thee with joy; he will rest in his love, he will joy over thee with singing" (Zeph. 3:17).

Because He loves us so, the Lord's joy derives from our having joy. This is what He really wants—for us to become the kind of beings that can have true joy. The Old Testament is full of that imagery. He has promised that we can have "joy and gladness and cheerful feasts" (Zech. 8:8, 19). Job speaks of the joy available to us, despite whatever sorrows we have either brought upon ourselves or had thrust upon us. This is a joy that comes because of the strength of the Lord: "In his neck remaineth strength, and sorrow is turned into joy before him" (Job 41:22). The Psalmist also speaks of the joy that comes from allowing God's strength to enable us: "But let all those that put their trust in thee rejoice: let them ever shout for joy, because thou defendest them: let them also that love thy name be joyful in thee" (Ps. 5:11). Note the tie between loving God and receiving joy.

Remember the image of Joshua the priest being clothed in filthy priestly garments? I believe that in one way or another that image applies to all of us. But so does the reverse image, wherein we are clothed as we would all like to be and receive the consequences thereof: "I [the Lord] will also clothe her priests with salvation: and her saints shall shout aloud for joy" (Ps. 132:16). As a result of what we become when the Lord will clothe us in righteousness, despite how often we have messed up, then "Let the saints be joyful in glory" (Ps. 149:5).

While this promised joy is real and God stands ready to help us become the kinds of beings who can experience it, so many of us doubt that we will. As Elder Jeffrey R. Holland pointed out that despite the fact that the Lord has spoken enough comforting words to cover the entire universe, we still see around us Latter-day Saints who are gloomy, unhappy, and worried—all because the Lord's words have not entered their hearts.[41] All of us need to believe Isaiah when he says, "Behold, God is my salvation; I will trust, and not be afraid: for the Lord Jehovah is my strength and my song; He also is become my salvation. Therefore with joy shall ye draw water out of the wells of salvation" (Isa. 12:2–3).

Though so much of Isaiah is about the wickedness of Israel and their impending doom, he also loved to dwell on the final, joyous state of Israel. Drawing on some of the imagery we have already seen in the Old Testament, two chapters of Isaiah sum up what the Lord hopes to do with Israel as a whole and with each Israelite individual. As we look at these chapters, let's try to feel and visualize what the Lord has in store for us.

Isaiah starts by describing the state of Israel (or you and me as Israelites) after their wickedness had led to corrective punishment by the Lord: "Sing, O barren, thou that didst not bear; break forth into singing, and cry aloud, thou that didst not travail with child: for more are the children of the desolate than the children of the married wife, saith the Lord" (Isa. 54:1). Here the Lord portrays scattered and punished Israel as a barren woman and paints a future of abundance and joy by promising her the offspring she so wants. However, as was the case with so many of the heroines of the Bible, that offspring came only after the sadness of being barren and the difficulty and pain of labor. So it is with Israel. God has punished her, but now that she is returning, her posterity and joy will be abundant.

Isaiah continues, "Enlarge the place of thy tent, and let them stretch forth the curtains of thine habitations: spare not, lengthen thy cords, and strengthen thy stakes; For thou shalt break forth on the right hand and on the left; and thy seed shall inherit the Gentiles, and make the desolate cities to be inhabited" (Isa. 54:2–3). This imagery is familiar to us, but as we understand its context it should take on new meaning. These verses continue the Lord's promise to barren and punished Israel. Her progeny will be so great that she will have to make her tent (in our day it would be her house) larger. As part of making the tent larger, Israel will need longer ropes and stronger stakes to hold the palatial tent in place. This has to happen because Israel will be growing on every side (both the right and the left) and will not consist not only of Israel, but the Gentiles who had once scourged them. Those cities that had been desolate as a part of God's punishment will now, with God's help, become full again. It is important that we realize this is happening literally for Israel, but also that we see how it applies to us. As we return to God, despite how often we have strayed, regardless of our numerous backslidings, He will make us greater than we have ever been. The past is not an issue. Regardless of what we have done, with God's help our future is greater than we can imagine.

This concept continues, and is even better illustrated, as God draws on the familiar imagery of a husband/wife relationship: "Fear not; for thou shalt not be ashamed: neither be thou confounded; for thou shalt not be put to shame: for thou shalt forget the shame of thy youth, and shalt not remember the reproach of thy widowhood any more. For thy Maker is thine husband; the Lord of hosts is his name; and thy Redeemer the Holy One of Israel; The God of the whole earth shall he be called" (Isa. 54:4–5). Note how eager God is to take away the shame we have earned for ourselves. We may have played the harlot but He is ready to overlook that incident, as Hosea did when Gomer returned. God wants us to remember who He is and that He has the power to do this—to bring us back.

God is not glossing over the fact that He has had to punish us. As He did with Gomer, He has hidden Himself from Israel (and from you and me) for a time but only as part of the process of coaxing us back: "For the Lord hath called thee as a woman forsaken and grieved in spirit, and a wife of youth, when thou wast refused, saith thy God. For a small moment have I forsaken thee; but with great mercies will I gather thee. In a little wrath I hid my face from thee for a moment; but with everlasting kindness will I have mercy on thee, saith the Lord thy Redeemer" (Isa. 54:6–8).

What beautiful imagery! The Lord clearly states that He had to hide Himself from us but is emphatic that His kindness towards us is everlasting and that He will still have mercy on us, whether we deserve it or not. The punishment or trials we experience are "for a small moment" (Isa. 54:7; see also D&C 121:7) but the kindness He will show us is everlasting. Sometimes it is hard to see it that way in the "moment," but God assures us this is the case.

We can better understand that perspective when we think of the history of humanity on the earth. God compares His wrath with Israel or with us to the time of the flood, a *short* period of horrific vengeance that has been followed by *countless generations* who have not experienced such a flood: "For this is as the waters of Noah unto me: for as I have sworn that the waters of Noah should no more go over the earth; so have I sworn that I would not be wroth with thee, nor rebuke thee. For the mountains shall depart, and the hills be removed; but my kindness shall not depart from thee, neither shall the covenant of my peace be removed, saith the Lord that hath mercy on thee" (Isa. 54:9–10).

We have already spoken of this last verse, but the passage takes on even more meaning when presented in context. After telling us that His mercy is everlasting (vs. 8), God shows us that His wrath is like the flood, which comes and then is done (vs. 9) and is followed by a covenant—kindness and mercy that will *never* depart. In our worst moments this should be a great comfort.

God follows the promise of His love and mercy with images of how the application of that mercy in our lives will make us more magnificent than we could have ever hoped for, despite how unlikely this may seem when things are difficult: "O thou afflicted, tossed with tempest, and not comforted, behold, I will lay thy stones with fair colours, and lay thy foundations with sapphires. And I will make thy windows of agates, and thy gates of carbuncles, and all thy borders of pleasant stones" (Isa. 54:11–12).

The Lord immediately follows this fanciful imagery of greatness with a promise that ties into His original symbolism of prosperity via progeny: "And all thy children shall be taught of the Lord; and great shall be the peace of thy children" (Isa. 54:13). Look at all the ways God is trying to describe what He wants to do for us. Despite the fact that we have estranged ourselves from God, He will bring us back into a faithful, loving relationship. He will give us so many children that we will need a larger tent. But this imagery is not enough; He promises that each element of it will get even better. Eventually it will not be a tent that we live in, but a city with precious gems and stones for windows, gates, foundations, and streets! We will not only have a large family, but our family will know of God and be blessed with peace!

God continues that imagery by demonstrating that He Himself will protect our new and happy selves: "In righteousness shalt thou be established: thou shalt be far from oppression; for thou shalt not fear: and from terror; for it shall not come near thee. Behold, they shall surely gather together, but not by me: whosoever shall gather together against thee shall fall for thy sake" (Isa. 54:14–15). In order to demonstrate His ability to provide this kind of protection, God reminds them of who He is, of His relationship to any who might want to harm Israel (or you), and states again that He will protect: "Behold, I have created the smith that bloweth the coals in the fire, and that bringeth forth an instrument for his work; and I have created the waster to destroy. No weapon that is formed against thee shall prosper; and every tongue that shall rise against thee in judgment thou shalt condemn. This is the heritage of the servants of the Lord, and their righteousness is of me, saith the Lord" (Isa. 54:16–17). After all, if God created those that make and use the weapons, He can surely keep them from using them to harm us. In other words, once we have decided we will return to God, He will take us back in, and there is nothing that can stop Him from making us into the kind of beings He wants us to become.

In case we were unsure whether we deserve such love and whether we merit being made into such wonderful beings, the Lord immediately reminds us that we do not need to deserve it or merit it. Using imagery that spoke eloquently to those who dwelt in a semi-arid land, God makes it clear that the gift He offers us can be ours regardless of our abilities: "Ho, every one that thirsteth, come ye to the waters, and He that hath no money; come ye, buy, and eat; yea, come, buy wine and milk without money and without price" (Isa. 55:1).

With this imagery comes a reminder that we should not, in a Gomer-like way, seek for rewards in places that we cannot really find them. Only God who can bring us true joy. "Wherefore do ye spend money for that which is not bread? and your labour for that which satisfieth not? hearken diligently unto me, and eat ye that which is good, and let your soul delight itself in fatness" (Isa. 55:2).

The Lord continues to encourage us to come to Him: "Incline your ear, and come unto me: hear, and your soul shall live; and I will make an everlasting covenant with you, even the sure mercies of David. Behold, I have given him for a witness to the people, a leader and commander to the people. Behold, thou shalt call a nation that thou knowest not, and nations that knew not thee shall run unto thee because of the Lord thy God, and for the Holy One of Israel; for he hath glorified thee" (Isa. 55:3–5). Here the Lord begs us to listen to Him. If we do so, He can give us the abundant life He has been speaking of. In order to help us picture this, He promises us the mercies of David.

The Lord took David, a little, unknown shepherd boy, and made Him into a wildly successful warrior and the greatest king Israel ever had. He established a covenant with David that is still in effect. As the Lord made David into a mighty king, He will do similar things for us. As He raised up David to deliver Israel, so will he, in the last days, raise up nations that ancient Israel had never heard of to protect Israel in the latter days. David specifically served as a type (witness) of what the Lord would do for us, both in bringing us saviors and in making us great.

All of this is ours if we will just return to God. The Lord issues a plea to do so: "Seek ye the Lord while he may be found, call ye upon him while he is near: Let the wicked forsake his way, and the unrighteous man his thoughts: and let him return unto the Lord, and he will have mercy upon him; and to our God, for he will abundantly pardon" (Isa. 55:6–7). What a poignant plea. As stated earlier, surely the Lord wants us to leave our wickedness behind. If we are willing to do so at any point, He will have mercy upon us; He will pardon us. Of this He leaves no doubt.

The Lord continues by saying something we have read before but that takes on new meaning when viewed in its proper context:

> For my thoughts are not your thoughts, neither are your ways my ways, saith the Lord.
> For as the heavens are higher than the earth, so are my ways higher than your ways, and my thoughts than your thoughts.

> For as the rain cometh down, and the snow from heaven, and returneth not thither, but watereth the earth, and maketh it bring forth and bud, that it may give seed to the sower, and bread to the eater:
>
> So shall my word be that goeth forth out of my mouth: it shall not return unto me void, but it shall accomplish that which I please, and it shall prosper in the thing whereto I sent it. (Isa. 55:8–11)

Viewed in this context, these verses become so much more powerful. They are designed to make emphatic the promises the Lord has just made. In other words, the Lord is saying that in case we are wondering whether we really can obtain His mercy, whether we really can be pardoned abundantly, we must remember that He thinks on a higher plane than we do. We may not understand how He could take us back. We may not be able to picture a God who is willing to heal us and make us great despite all that we have done and become. It may be unthinkable to us that He could exalt such a being as you or me. But God is telling us that we just don't understand—we can't possibly comprehend things the way He does. And to make sure we really get it, He tells us that if He says something, He means it. He does not say things that will not happen. He doesn't speak empty words. If He tells you He will have mercy, if He says He will pardon, if He promises He will make us great, if He covenants to exalt us, we can be absolutely sure that He will do it. God means what He says. He never speaks empty words.

With that firm reminder, He gives us one last image of what He intends to do with us: "For ye shall go out with joy, and be led forth with peace: the mountains and the hills shall break forth before you into singing, and all the trees of the field shall clap their hands. Instead of the thorn shall come up the fir tree, and instead of the brier shall come up the myrtle tree: and it shall be to the Lord for a name, for an everlasting sign that shall not be cut off" (Isa. 55:12–13). Can you picture this? The Lord is promising to reverse the effects of the Fall when He speaks of turning thorns and briers into beautiful trees. He promises us that our peace and joy will be so great that even the mountains and hills will sing and the trees will clap. God, who has just told us that if He says it He means it, promises that He will turn us into beings that are more full of joy and peace than we can possibly comprehend.

The Lord will take us back, He will make us into such beings. The oft-repeated plea to return to Him, the never-ending willingness to bring us home, the incessant extension of grace and second chances pervade the Old Testament and should pervade our lives, filling us with joy. No matter how often we have messed up, regardless of how far we backslide, however weak and foolish we are, irrespective of how much we have struggled and continue to fail in our strivings, He can make us into a new, light-filled, perfect creature capable of unfathomable joy. He paid the price to make it possible if we will only return to Him: "And the ransomed of the Lord shall return, and come to Zion with songs and everlasting joy upon their heads: they shall obtain joy and gladness, and sorrow and sighing shall flee away" (Isa. 35:10).

As Paul taught, "In all these things we are more than conquerors through him that loved us. For I am persuaded, that neither death, nor life, nor angels, nor principalities, nor powers, nor things present, nor things to come, nor height, nor depth, nor any creature, shall be able to separate us from the love of God, which is in Christ Jesus our Lord" (Rom. 8:37–39).

Because of His ardent love for us, God compares us to His bride and fully accepts us when we return to Him—and the joy follows. "The voice of joy, and the voice of gladness, the voice of the bridegroom, and the voice of the bride, the voice of them that shall say, Praise the Lord of hosts: for the Lord *is* good; for his mercy endureth for ever" (Jer. 33:11). Oh, how the Lord loves us!

ENDNOTES

1 Spencer W. Kimball, "A Special Message to All Latter-day Saints," *Ensign*, Nov. 1980, 94.

2 Jeffrey R. Holland, "Come and See," *Liahona*, Aug. 1998, 44.

3 John H. Groberg, "The Power of God's Love," *Liahona*, Nov. 2004, 9–11.

4 Neal A. Maxwell, *Sermons Not Spoken* (Salt Lake City: Bookcraft, 1985), 25–26.

5 Russell M. Nelson, "Jesus Christ—the Master Healer," *Ensign*, Nov. 2005, 87.

6 Boyd K. Packer, *Mine Errand From the Lord* (Salt Lake City: Deseret Book, 2008), 59.

7 *Journal of Discourses*, 19:159–160.

8 Thomas S. Monson, "Looking Back and Moving Forward," *Ensign*, May 2008, 90.

9 Dieter F. Uchtdorf, "Point of Safe Return," *Ensign*, May 2007, 99.

10 Ibid., 101.

11 Jeffrey R. Holland, "Come and See," *Liahona*, Aug. 1998, 44.

12 D. Chad Richardson, "Forgiving Oneself," *Ensign*, March 2007, 30–33.

13 "O Savior, Thou Who Wearest a Crown," *Hymns,* 197.

14 "Chapter 35: Redemption for the Dead," in *Teachings of Presidents of the Church: Joseph Smith* (Salt Lake City: The Church of Jesus Christ of Latter-day Saints, 2007), 401–411.

15 My gratitude to Heide Showalter for showing this to me.

16 Dieter F. Uchtdorf, "The Way of the Disciple," *Liahona*, May 2009, 75–78.

17 Jeffrey R. Holland, "Come and See," *Liahona,* Aug. 1998, 44.

18 Boyd K. Packer, *Mine Errand from the Lord* (Salt Lake City: Deseret Book, 2008), 37.

19 Joseph B. Wirthlin, "The Great Commandment," *Ensign,* Nov. 2007, 29–30.

20 Thomas S. Monson, "Tears, Trials, Trust, Testimony," *Ensign,* Sept. 1997, 2.

21 Of all sources, the Veggie Tales Movie about Jonah helped to clarify this for me.

22 Neal A. Maxwell, "Thanks Be to God," *Ensign,* July 1982, 51.

23 Neal A. Maxwell, "It's Service, Not Status, That Counts," *Ensign,* July 1975, 7.

24 Jeffrey R. Holland, "Come and See," *Liahona,* Aug. 1998, 44.

25 D. Todd Christofferson, "The Divine Gift of Repentance," *Ensign,* Nov. 2011, 38–41.

26 Ibid.

27 For a longer version of this section, see Kerry Muhlestein, "Believing in the Atoning Power of Christ," in *Covenants, Prophecies, and Hymns of the Old Testament,* Victor Ludlow, ed. (Provo, UT: Brigham Young University Press, 2001), 89–100.

28 Ibid., 169.

29 Kent P. Jackson, comp., ed., *Joseph Smith's Commentary on the Bible* (Salt Lake City: Deseret Book Company, 1994), 29.

30 For more on this idea, see Stephen E. Robinson, *Believing Christ* (Salt Lake City: Deseret Book Company, 1992), 9.

31 S. Kent Brown, "Trust in the Lord: Exodus and Faith," *The Old Testament and the Latter-day Saints* (Salt Lake City: Randall Book Company, 1986), 93, also writes of this.

32 Ned B. Roueché, "Feed My Sheep," *Ensign,* Nov. 2004, 30.

33 Dieter F. Uchtdorf, "You Matter to Him," *Ensign,* Nov. 2011, 19–22.

34 C.S. Lewis, *Mere Christianity* (San Francisco: Harper Collins Publishers, 1952), 153.

35 David A. Bednar, "Ye Must Be Born Again," *Ensign,* May 2007, 19–22

36 Stephen R. Covey, *Spiritual Roots of Human Relations* (Salt Lake City: Deseret Book, 1970), 93.

37 Ezra Taft Benson, "Jesus Christ—Gifts and Expectations," *The New Era*, May 1975, 2.

38 *Teachings of the Prophet Joseph Smith*, sel. Joseph Fielding Smith (Salt Lake City: Deseret Book, 1977), 241.

39 Anne C. Pingree, "To Look, Reach, and Come unto Christ," *Ensign,* Nov. 2006, 115.

40 Original quote by Joseph F. Smith in Boyd K. Packer, "The Brilliant Morning of Forgiveness," *New Era*, Apr. 2005, 4.

41 Jeffrey R. Holland, "Come and See," *Liahona*, Aug. 1998, 44.

SCRIPTURE INDEX

ABOUT THE AUTHOR

Dr. Kerry Muhlestein is an associate professor of ancient scripture and ancient Near Eastern studies at Brigham Young University, where he is the associate chair of the Department of Ancient Scripture. He received his B.S. cum laude from BYU in psychology with a Hebrew minor. In order to learn Hebrew, he spent time at the BYU Jerusalem Center for Near Eastern Studies in the intensive Hebrew program. He received an M.A. in ancient Near Eastern studies from BYU and then his Ph.D. from UCLA in Egyptology.

He has taught courses in Hebrew and religion at BYU and UVU; history at Cal Poly Pomona and UCLA; and religion and history at BYU–Hawaii. He is involved with the American Research Center in Egypt and as a master's degree student at BYU he worked on the Dead Sea Scrolls database project. He was also instrumental in arranging for the first-ever Egyptology Conference in Hawaii at BYU–Hawaii. He often travels to Egypt, where he heads up the BYU Egypt Excavation Project.

Dr. Muhlestein focuses mainly on ancient Egypt, the Hebrew Bible, and the Pearl of Great Price. His research focuses on the texts and iconography of Egyptian religion, international contact between ancient Egypt and her neighbors, the Egyptian juridical process, Egyptian literature, and the overlap of the Biblical and Egyptian worlds, including the ancient and modern history of the Pearl of Great Price.

He and his wife, Julianne, have six children. He and his family spent a year in Jerusalem while he taught at the BYU Jerusalem Center for Near Eastern Studies.

Photo by Zane W. Hamilton; for information, visit www.zham61.wix.com/zane-w-hamilton